Hash

Hash

Published by The Conrad Press Ltd. in the United Kingdom 2023

Tel: +44(0)1227 472 874

www.theconradpress.com
info@theconradpress.com

ISBN 978-1-915494-89-4

Copyright © F. Ritchie 2023
All rights reserved.

Typesetting by Michelle Emerson michelleemerson.co.uk

Cover design by Hendrick Sultana

The Conrad Press logo was designed by Maria Priestley

Printed and bound in Great Britain by Clays Ltd, Elcograf S.p.A.

Hash

F. Ritchie

Preface

When I was first introduced to Pommie, the man standing before me was tall and lean, with dancing bright bluey-grey eyes, and incredibly personable. He had impeccable manners, was quick to smile and after only five minutes chatting to him, it was clear he was a very intelligent person.

He had popped around from his friend's next door wondering if I would write a book about his antics in Holland in the early 1990s.

Antics!

He had been a violent, savage, vicious member of a gang, who were highly organised, brutal kidnappers and expert torturers.

That caught my attention.

So, we agreed to meet once a week for an hour or so, while Pommie spoke about his extraordinary experiences.

I kept interrupting him because some of what he said didn't make sense. But then I didn't have the mind of a hardened criminal. I was fascinated with the detail of the clothing they wore and huge arsenal they had. Equally, the intricate planning to ensure the gang got their desired results.

I can only write from Pommie's perspective. Any gang member still alive that reads this, will doubtless have a completely different view or memory. I can only recount the tale of *Hash* from the man who was there.

Latterly, they were given a title, but the gang never had a name while they were working, they really did have better things to do with their time.

Their notoriety still fascinates people in Holland today, because nobody knows how they got away with it. Was there a powerful or influential person they had the drop on, or was it down to their slick preparation and clever moves?

I have no idea why Pommie chose me to relate this story, or why he felt the time was right for people to hear his point of view. Perhaps it's because none of the gang have talked about their involvement with anyone else before, but their silence still provokes curiosity and intrigue about what actually went on.

The gang's names aren't real, but people will know who they are, as doubtless old hacks and coppers will too. They would never get away with it today, and even though they were a bunch of

intensely fierce and sadistic men, there is something deep down that you can't help admiring them for.
   I think it's the stuff of movies.

October 2023 - F. Ritchie

CHAPTER ONE

'What do you mean, it didn't click?' I was staring at one of the best robbers in Europe, unable to comprehend what he meant.

'Just that. It didn't click.'

'Surely you don't mean there isn't an alarm on this place?'

'No, and there's no security cameras either.'

With that, Verdun slowly stuck his head back through the gap on the wooden side panel of the storage unit he had just removed with a saw.

His smile said it all. We had just broken into a police warehouse where there were thousands of five-kilogram tins of apricots that we were keen to remove. It seemed that all the patient preparation of the last twelve months had been worth the effort.

Chapter Two

It was early in 1993 when Leon had a visit from Dom.

Leon saw himself as the leader of the gang and we let him carry on with this belief because it wasn't worth the hassle of arguing with him. His ego was big enough to handle it, and someone needed to be approachable, so we just let him get on with it. Leon wanted the reputation of being a big-time player but didn't fully recognise that we could work equally well as a team without him.

Dom was an unhappy employee who worked for a local trucking company based in South West Holland.

Most of our leads came from people like Dom. They saw their bosses making a lot of money and wanted a share of it. They were not bright enough to earn it for themselves and they resented others who did. Once they'd plucked up the courage to make contact with one of the gang, usually Leon, they were happy to grass up their bosses to get a cut of the action.

To my recollection, Leon had met Dom on at least three occasions, so we weren't expecting to get anything out of him. Dom hadn't got any solid leads, and only thought some hash deal might be going down, so we were surprised when Leon contacted us for a meeting.

Eight of us turned up at his house to hear what, if anything, the plan was. It was apparent that Dom's bosses regularly brought shipments of hash from places like Morocco or Afghanistan into either Holland or Belgium. They had many warehouses across Holland which fronted a legitimate catering business, so their trucks were a familiar sight on the roads.

The truck drivers working for this company stood to get a huge amount of cash if they moved the hash from a port to an allotted site. Dom had never been approached to do this in the five years he'd worked for them, so his resentment had been building for some time. He was married with two small children, and he wanted to make a better life for them all. He could see other employees doing well and he desperately wanted a part of the action.

The fact he was so severely dyslexic that he was barely able to read or write and couldn't understand a map, wasn't something he considered to be a major handicap. Five years' loyalty surely meant something, so in a fit of pique, he made an approach to Leon in a small coffee bar in the middle of town.

Looking back, if it hadn't been for Leon, I would never have made it into the gang in the first place. I was a friend of Chris, who I met when we both left the French Foreign Legion on the same day after three years' service. We got on immediately as we both understood what it was like to live with danger and the importance of always having a comrade's back.

I spent a few weeks knocking about with Chris around Europe, before finding my way back to England where I worked as a car mechanic. I was good at the job but, after a few months, I started to get restless. I decided to make an approach to the Kuwaiti Embassy as there was a war raging at the time and they were looking for trained militia to help fight their cause.

They were keen to accept anyone foolish enough to take up the challenge and were prepared to pay handsomely for that service. The fact that you were unlikely to survive a year was a mere inconvenience. The wages were so good that I phoned Chris and arranged to meet him in Holland a couple of days later, thinking he might want to join me.

It appeared that Chris had already joined a gang with his brother and, despite my best sales technique, he said he would stay with them as he reckoned his chances of survival in Holland would be a lot higher than in Kuwait. Also, his girlfriend was pregnant, and he really wanted to stay close to her.

However, given my skills, he thought I would really fit in with the gang and he would see if they would let me join. He suggested I go back to England and wait for his call. This wasn't a willy-nilly thing, being invited to join the gang. They were very close-knit, merciless, fearless and ruthless. Certainly not people to mess around with.

So I went back to England and waited impatiently to hear from Chris.

It took a lot longer than I thought before he got in touch. I'm convinced I wouldn't have heard from him for at least a year or two, had it not been for the gang finding themselves two men down. Leon had managed to get himself kidnapped, and Verdun had got himself shot.

It happened that Leon and Verdun had almost pulled off a rip deal. These are deals where you steal either money or drugs or both, from another gang. The rip deal had taken place in Maastricht. Leon had come to an agreement to buy two hundred kilos of hash from the Yugoslavs. Stupidly, and more importantly, against all the pleas of the other gang members, he had decided to pay for this hash with fake American dollars.

The Yugoslavs were a rival gang. We had given them this generic name because the top guys were Yugoslavian. We respected each other's patch but, although we knew of them, we didn't need or, in fact, want to know anything about them.

The middleman for the assignment was a gypsy who had organised the deal between the two gangs. He was responsible for taking the dollars from Leon and the hash from the Yugoslavs, ensuring a nice bonus for himself for a job well done. The gypsy did not notice that the dollars were counterfeit so, when the Yugoslavs turned up at his house to collect the cash, they were more than a little upset. They decided to kidnap him and took him to a nearby gypsy camp for a chat. They strongly recommended that he called Leon to arrange a meeting. This was set for the following day. Leon and Verdun went on their own, without telling any of the gang where or when they were going.

As stupid decisions go, this has got to be right up there. Mind you, if Leon hadn't gone, I wouldn't have had a call from Chris to fly to Holland and help save their sorry backsides.

So, Leon and Verdun piled up at the gypsy camp and were immediately struck by the lack of women and children who are normally running about outside. Only men were visible and most of them were keenly watching their arrival.

There was a brand new BMW on the site. The boot was open and you could see that the back seat was folded down. This was clearly out of the ordinary but, regardless, Leon and Verdun headed to the caravan where they had agreed to meet. The gypsy middleman offered them coffee and, as Leon was midway to sitting down, the Yugoslavs pounced on him.

They realised very quickly that they weren't going to get ambushed by the rest of our gang as there was clearly no back up. I bet they couldn't believe their luck.

Just as Leon was pounced on, someone pulled a gun and shot Verdun.

In the split second that he saw the gun and realised what was happening, Verdun turned to his left to reach for his pistol, but not quickly enough, as the bullet hit him. He dropped to the deck, unconscious and bleeding profusely. As far as anyone could tell, he was dead. The gang stepped over him and drove off with Leon.

They took him to a warehouse in Amsterdam in the back of the BMW. Apparently, when Leon saw Verdun had been shot, the colour drained from his face as he truly believed they had killed him, so now he had grounds to fear for his own life.

On arrival at the warehouse Leon recognised one of the kidnappers. His name was Sammy Klepper, a well-known partner of Johannes Mieremet, who was wildly feared in the Amsterdam underworld.

This duo, incidentally, were known as Spic and Span due to the incredibly efficient, effective, and undetectable manner in which they got rid of their opponents.

However, they were not exactly professionals when it came to kidnapping. They started to torture Leon by putting electrodes onto his testicles. There were also four or five pit bull terriers at the warehouse, all keen to get a bite out of him. They blindfolded him and shot a bullet from a gun next to his ear into a bucket of sand. Further mental torture included placing a six-shooter against his head and firing. He had been shown that there was only one bullet, so it was potluck if he lived or died.

Meanwhile, back at the gypsy camp the acting middleman had called an ambulance, and Verdun had been taken to hospital. He was treated for a torn pectoralis major muscle and a flesh wound where the bullet had passed through. When he had twisted his body to reach his gun, his speedy reflex reaction had actually saved his life. He was discharged from hospital six days later.

Having Leon out of the picture and Verdun in hospital, the gang needed more help so, with reluctance, they asked Chris to make a call to me. This would serve two purposes. Firstly, they knew they would have a fearless man who was a crack shot on their team and, secondly, it would stop Chris's nagging for me to join the gang.

Chapter Three

It was late morning when I got the call from Chris, and he spoke with such urgency about the situation, that I knew I had to leave immediately.

My father owned the garage where I worked, so it made leaving quickly a lot easier.

Although he wasn't happy, Dad understood and, after popping home to pack a bag, I got myself to London City Airport, flew to Holland, and arrived at Chris's house in under two hours.

There were no introductions. I was handed a semi-automatic handgun, which I checked was safe and tucked into the waistband of my jeans. The remaining gang were in three cars outside. Chris got into one separate from me, and we drove into the Yugoslav territory.

We had no idea where the gang members lived but we knew that, leading up to any major job, men tended to let their hair and beards grow. You would be amazed how drastically different you look afterwards with a haircut, but it must not be a shoddy haircut. A poor haircut can make you stand out, which is the last thing you want, so it needs to be a good style and professionally done.

We suspected some of the Yugoslav kidnappers were likely to want to change their appearance, so we travelled to their territory in Amsterdam and headed to an area of shops that had a few up-market hairdressers and waited patiently for our mark. We struck gold on the third day.

As the guy left the barbers, eight of us leapt from our cars. He recognised who we were and that we were after him. He headed for the nearby shopping centre, running like his life depended on it. Which, of course, it did.

We all ran with our guns drawn and, luckily, it wasn't long before we caught up with him. Once trapped, someone grabbed his phone so he couldn't warn anyone, and his gun, so he couldn't harm anyone. More importantly, we had his mobile contacts, and all of his personal ID.

People shopping in the mall looked shocked at our sudden appearance and the urgency of the chase, but they simply got out of the way, most probably assuming we were the police.

We didn't want to look at his ugly face, so we put a bag over his head, shoved him in the boot of a car and drove off. We felt pretty confident that his gang would want him back so, for safe keeping, he was taken to Leon's garage.

Calling from the kidnapees' mobile, we informed the Yugoslavs we had their boy. We had slapped him around a bit but not tortured him, for two main reasons. First, they would inflict an equal measure of punishment on Leon and second, we wanted to be more honourable than they were.

Frankly, neither of the gangs wanted the hassle. So a deal was struck and both men were released, relatively unharmed, within twenty-four hours of our phone call.

Overnight our gang had their old mob back and I was now part of their group. The Yugoslavs realised it was way too much hassle for them to get the hash back so, despite the pain and heartache, the deal had eventually proven to be profitable and successful.

I didn't know what the gang thought of me, but I certainly got the feeling that I was a hugely resented outsider.

Chapter Four

The gang had been established for a few years and were expert bank robbers. However, security improvements, the development of modern technology, and an increasing concern about harming a member of public, meant a change of plan was needed so, just as I joined them, they had turned their skills to carrying out rip deals.

The secret of success with our group was that it worked in a slightly different way to other gangs. We had a floating number in our team of between ten and fifteen men. A majority needed to agree to do a job and, once successfully completed, the profits were split equally between however many got involved in the heist in the first place.

With no leader we were a much greater threat. Should one of us get into trouble, the rest of the gang would come to the rescue. If you threatened one of us, you threatened all of us.

As the newest and most resented member I had to prove myself. I would only be paid a salary for the first two jobs we did, and only if I made the cut, would I then be paid an equal share.

Having been in the French Foreign Legion I knew my way around almost all gun models, grenades and ammunition. I was also a good car mechanic, so felt I could add value to the team.

The first two jobs went like a dream, and although I still couldn't understand what they were saying – it really did sound like double Dutch – it was decided that the Pommie could stay.

Chapter Five

Mick was the most intelligent criminal I had ever met, and a great generator of wealth, albeit through nefarious activities. He was an engineer and spoke several languages. He was also an expert in explosives.

He was extremely fit and broad, six feet seven without an ounce of fat on him.

I met Mick while the gang was surrounding a local nightclub with a cordon of police and dog handlers round us. We were waiting for the police inside the club to release one of our gang, along with a close criminal associate.

While we were waiting, Mick had decided to wind up a nearby police dog which was a Belgian Alsatian. The dog wound Mick up and vice versa. With one huge lunge the dog leapt forward and bit Mick on the groin. I burst out laughing. He said he thought I was the most arrogant fuck he'd ever met, to which I replied, 'ditto'. He must have been in real pain, but that was the beginning of our friendship and, if it were not for him, we would never have got started in the ecstasy business.

Anyway, Mick would visit various cafés around the South West region that the gang controlled. He would just sit, drink coffee and listen. The more familiar a sight he became, the more confident people were to approach him and share any news they may have had about a hash deal in the pipeline.

We didn't take on every job but, when we did and succeeded, Mick would ensure the grass got a share of our profits. It boosted confidence for others to come forward. Let's face it, if you grass to the police, you get paid nothing, but talking to a gang could reap financial rewards.

Most people who approached us would invariably be holding a grudge or fed up with their job, or occasionally a husband. One fine example was a bloke called Bill Raisin.

I'm sure there are a lot of clever men in this world who have affairs and their wives never find out. However, if you are a low life fool who thinks he's a big man because he makes ecstasy pills and has good money to spend on mistresses, then you'd better think again. It just so happened that Bill's wife had had more than enough of her husband's shenanigans so, instead of confronting him and having a row, she confronted Mick and negotiated a deal. She would receive twenty percent of anything we managed to take from her husband.

They lived in a rather palatial house that had a separate garage which, according to his wife, was pretty much full of ecstasy pills, mixing agents and chemicals. There were also some guns, the machine to make the tablets, money from the pills he'd already sold, and virtually all of his contacts in a Filofax.

We went to do a recce of the house to ensure we didn't come across anything unexpected. Then we planned where to park the cars without them being spotted, as the element of surprise is a key advantage.

His wife gave us the heads up a few days later, when Bill was in the house watching television, and not in the garage.

About ten of the gang assembled at Bill's home and surrounded it. Verdun and I crept to the glass-fronted patio door which he smashed with a crowbar. He then ran the crowbar around the inside frame of the door to remove any jagged glass, so we didn't get cut as we ran in. Bill knew this was either a gang or police raid and he immediately jumped to his feet and fled upstairs to grab a gun from a bedroom. By now, I had run around to the foot of the stairs and aimed my gun upwards.

The red dot from my semi-automatic pistol that appeared on Bill's chest was enough for him to give in. He had been over-powered and outnumbered all within five minutes of us smashing his door in. Had he been armed downstairs when we entered and worked out quickly that we weren't the police, he would have shot us dead. Luckily, he wasn't, and he didn't.

We had to play the game, so someone grabbed his wife and shoved her into the back of a car, while Bill was dragged into the boot of another. Both were driven to the safe house. His wife sat in a comfortable chair we had in the garage and watched VHS tapes to pass the time. Leon ran around after her, making her hot chocolate and serving biscuits. Bill was slightly less comfortable, but he wasn't going to come to any harm, as we just needed him out of the way long enough to steal everything he had.

We released his wife a few hours before him, and he never suspected she had set him up. A couple of points to note are that we only ever took things that people were criminally liable for. Crooks are never going to go to the police to say their ecstasy pills, gear and money have been stolen. However, if you took something they personally owned, like the family car, chances are they would grass on you.

In amongst the chemicals in Bill's garage was a mixing agent called Avicel. For those who might have a fleeting interest, Avicel is the trade name for microcrystalline cellulose that has been partially hydrolysed with acid and reduced to a fine powder to be used as a fat replacer.

It disperses in water and has the properties of a gum. It is used in oily foods such as cheese and peanut butter, as well as in syrups and honey, sauces and dressings. The beauty of it is that it releases a chemical compound slowly into the human system, so it doesn't harm people. Sadly, because it was known to be used in the making of ecstasy, the European Medicines Agency changed its status. This meant Avicel went from being readily available to being a licensed product, therefore making it much harder to get hold of.

Why people thought that banning Avicel would prevent anyone manufacturing ecstasy is beyond me. Instead, they used any other crap that was available, which made the pills unstable and, as a result, people started to die. Our intention all along was to make money, never to kill anyone. It beggars belief really.

So, Bill provided us with some very sought-after Avicel, which we stored safely for another day.

The pills were kept in various places across our patch. They were so well hidden, it was virtually impossible for anyone to find them. The police had almost worked out that we only ever got together as a gang when we were planning a rip deal or moving our stock to sell it. Their best bet to apprehend us was to spot us as a group and then keep tabs on us.

They usually only managed this by sheer luck, but occasionally when something went down their suspicions were enough for them to keep an eye on at least one of us, assuming they could actually find one of us, of course.

The one thing I never did was to ignore my instincts. With my experience as a Legionnaire, it wasn't difficult to spot police officers who were trying to look inconspicuous, so I always knew when we were under surveillance.

One particular day we met up with the intention of selling some hash. Six of us travelled in three cars. The hash was in the front car, with the back-up vehicles being used as a distraction, or to deviate any problems that might arise. I was paired with Buck, driving a 2L 16V Vauxhall Calibra and bringing up the rear. It was obvious within a mile of setting off that we were being followed. I informed the two leading cars by walkie-talkie of this fact.

Buck was a super-intelligent bloke, and he was probably the calmest person in our group. He was also a good shot, a good fighter and genuinely funny. His one flaw was that he was a terrible driver. He was so bad, in fact, I wouldn't let him drive me anywhere and I actually spent many hours teaching him how to drive properly. In all the time he was part of the gang he never drove a getaway car.

The police didn't know whether we had any drugs with us or if were planning to go and pick some up. We deliberately drove to an area near a housing estate because it happened to be where Chris lived. The road was one-way and situated between two dykes which meant there was no possibility that we could be overtaken.

An unmarked police car was at least a hundred metres behind us. The officers probably couldn't believe their luck that they had come across so many of the gang in one place. Needless to say, their suspicions were aroused that we must be up to no good. They genuinely thought we wouldn't spot them. God loves a trier.

I started to slow down and then came to a juddering halt. Buck and I slowly got out of the car, opened the bonnet and started looking under it while studiously rubbing our chins. Enough minutes had passed to allow the front two cars a clear getaway. Eventually, I strolled up to the police car to address the two men inside, both sitting bolt upright wearing sparkling new white suit shirts. They might as well have been in full uniform with a blue flashing light on the roof.

My opening gambit was to tell them I knew they were coppers and to ask them if they had any tools in the boot that might help us fix our car. They were unimpressed and oddly uncooperative, but they didn't deny they were police.

We ambled back to my car and set off in a completely different direction to where we had planned to sell the hash. We were delighted and amused to see the trailing coppers drive towards Chris's house, in the strong belief that that was where the front cars had headed. Buck and I went to a café, had a nice cup of tea and caught up with the rest of the lads later that evening.

Chapter Six

After the third meeting between Leon and Dom, we agreed to take him on board. It was a bit of a long shot because he'd never been selected to drive the hash consignments from a dock to a warehouse before and, after five years being employed as a truck driver, we weren't entirely convinced that he ever would.

As I said before, Dom was severely dyslexic, but he did have a photographic memory. He knew where the warehouses were located across Holland, most of which had been used at one point or another to store the large quantities of illegal hash being imported.

Eight of us bought into the deal and we agreed on a twenty-five percent cut to Dom. We just had to work out some sort of plan so that he could inform us when something was going down.

The initial idea was to get information about the location of the warehouses. The only way to do this was to drive Dom around on his days off. That task fell on to my shoulders as my wife lived in England, while the other gang members either had wives, girlfriends, or both, to cope with. I was the Pommie patsy.

There were several rules we stuck to. Simple things, but pretty important to ensure our success.

First and foremost, we agreed not to seriously harm or kill anyone, not even a potential enemy. If you deal in drugs and people get hurt, then you are not doing your job properly. The police put much more effort into catching dealers who use extreme violence or kill someone.

We also agreed that we would only deal in hash or cannabis, or whatever drug fell below the Class As, such as cocaine. We always told the truth and were up front with each other. Probably the biggest advantage was our planning. We really planned ahead, no matter how long it took because good planning does reap rewards.

Other smaller details included remembering everyone's phone numbers. We never wrote anything down as it could be used as evidence. We never sold a gun, even if it hadn't been used. We were not easy to identify as we purposely had no tattoos or piercings. We never kept an address book or mobile phone as these contain contact details which would be useful to other people.

We each had our own car, which was legally owned by each gang member and was always filled with fuel. Each tyre on the car was the same model and tread and we made sure each vehicle was checked regularly for water and oil. After all, this was the only source of transport, so you had to know your car wasn't going to fail you.

When planning a job, it was vital to know exactly where the police stations, helipads, hospitals and schools were located, as these had to be avoided. Also, we had to know where the one-way streets and dead ends were. We always had at least five escape routes, so if one was blocked, we had four more to fall back on.

People also believe what they see, so a rip deal needs to look like a fracas. If people are watching from a distance and witness ten seconds of action, it's a disturbance. If they see a gun, it's an armed robbery. Finally, and probably most importantly, don't die through lack of bullets.

Chapter Seven

Dom and I used to meet at a local railway station.

I knew which train he would be coming in on. It was usually on a Saturday morning so there was a reasonable amount of activity. I would watch through binoculars so I could see if he left the train and then anticipate when he would be coming through the exit. We didn't communicate at all, so I could never assume he would be on the train to start with.

I would pull up at the station door the exact moment he walked through it. Dom would put on his seat belt as he got into the passenger seat, so we were away from the station within a couple of seconds.

To any observer we were just two blokes who were mates, probably going to have a pint and watch the football later.

I drove while he directed, as he knew exactly where to go. I never spoke to him, but if he wanted to chat then that was down to him. He would say when we were close to a warehouse and which side of the road it was located. I would drive straight past it, and neither of us would turn our heads to look. When I drove back to the train station, I avoided passing the warehouse for a second time.

Once home, I would mark it on a map with codes and, once the gang knew the code by heart, I would destroy the map.

Dom and I rarely missed a weekend. Some journeys took as little as fifteen minutes, while others took hours.

This went on for a year and, frankly, we were beginning to wonder if anything was ever going to come of it.

Then one evening Leon's phone rang.

Chapter Eight

Dom had been selected to drive that day because, at the very last minute, one of the usual blokes had suddenly fallen sick. He happened to be working at the warehouse where Dom was on duty, so they had almost no choice but to ask him to stand in.

The two bosses approached him about an hour before the end of his shift and asked if he wanted to earn himself a quick five thousand. The second he agreed, they took his mobile from him and, at the appointed time, they sat him in a van between them and drove him to Antwerp harbour.

His instructions were to meet the truck from the ship and take over the driving. There were two identical company trucks on board and all he had to do was follow the other lorry to an undisclosed place. His bosses were not permitted to enter a particular part of the port, so they dropped him off and returned to Holland to one of their warehouses to await the arrival of tins of apricots.

In the short period of time that he was

unaccompanied, Dom had managed to get a call in to Leon, unobserved by the fellow driver who was collecting the other truck. It was a huge risk for him to take but, as the potential financial reward for him was so great, it was more than worth the gamble. The conversation would have been one word, and a second long.

You have to bear in mind that this was the early 1990s when there weren't many mobile phones around and we didn't use any form of communication that could trace us.

Leon paged us all with a code. No one but the gang knew what these codes meant and we changed them frequently, sometimes after forty-eight hours or, very occasionally, it could be as long as ten days. The code was associated with a meeting point so, as soon as you got it, you dropped everything and simply turned up at the designated place as quickly as humanly possible.

Within minutes after Dom had made the call to Leon, we were in four cars driving as fast as we could possibly go towards Antwerp docks.

Chapter Nine

Each of the gang had skills they brought to the party and there were several nationalities between us. Understanding a different language was never a problem because, invariably, one of us would be fluent in it.

It was helpful to have inside knowledge as to how the police worked so, as we had an ex-copper as part of the team, it gave us a fresh understanding as to how to think like police. No one ever asked questions as to how the gang acquired stuff. It was simply accepted that genuine police uniforms, including the boots, and a fair amount of weapons and ammunition were always available and obviously helped our cause.

Bearing in mind that our criminality was our livelihood, none of us could afford for anything to go wrong, so we had to plan our deals very carefully because, if one of us failed, the others might not have an income for several months. The best burglar in Holland was Verdun. There wasn't anything he couldn't break into at an alarming speed. Verdun had the view that if you took someone else's money, especially if it had been acquired illegally, or removed it from a bank without hurting anyone, then that was fair game. Bank robbing was a lot easier back then as, with no on-line banking and very few debit cards, cash was king and there was plenty of it about if you knew how to get your hands on it.

I joined the gang just as they had made the decision that raiding banks was becoming too risky, but they did share the secrets of how they planned their robberies.

The idea was to find a bank in a town rather than one in a city, as these smaller banks had yet to embrace how to fully protect themselves and their money.

The gang would select a bank, somewhere like Rotterdam. For several weeks prior to the break in, they would drive around the whole area within a minimum of a five-mile radius. All roads were memorised, so they knew where the schools, police stations, hospitals, dead ends, and one-way systems were. You do not want to find yourself being pursued only then to discover that you are heading towards a police station you hadn't noticed before.

They also watched and followed the habits of the bank employees so they knew what they looked like, where they lived, what car they drove, what their spouse and children looked like and what time they left for work in the morning.

There are no short cuts in meticulous planning, so the tiniest of details were thought through and no attempt was made to go ahead with a break-in until they were all completely satisfied that they had achieved what they referred to as the six Ps: Perfect Planning Prevents Piss Poor Performance.

They would use a different car each time they went on a surveillance trip, never stopping to double check something or make notes. The whole area was memorised, and they were never on the road for long periods as they didn't want to draw attention to themselves. On the day of the robbery the getaway car would be legitimately hired, and then false number plates were attached.

The break-ins were planned in the winter months as it was dark by four in the afternoon. When people went home and settled down for the evening, they would usually close their curtains and not go out again until the next day.

It's funny how you don't think about these things, but very few people look up when they are out shopping on a High Street. They might if a low flying plane or helicopter appeared, but generally people don't look at rooftops, especially when it starts to get dark.

So, once the bank closed for the day, three of the

gang would break in through the roof. Back in the 1980s, only the bank itself was alarmed and not areas like roof space. Once in, and obviously unheard, they would remove all the surfaces between their floor and the bank ceiling and, once completely satisfied there was only a thin area to break through, they would settle down for the night. As part of their due diligence, the gang would have established when the best day would be to break in. It might be that the quietest day was Monday, in which case they would spend the weekend in the roof space. Some banks may have fewer staff on a Tuesday, or there may be more money in the safe on a Thursday. Whatever the situation, the gang set itself up for as little risk and as much cash as possible.

In the morning the staff would enter the bank, probably half an hour before opening to the public. They would then deactivate all the alarms and open the safe in order to stock the tills. The scrupulous planning meant that the gang knew when the last staff member would arrive, and it was at that point that the three of them would drop through the ceiling.

Understanding human nature, the gang knew that no one would panic in the first thirty seconds as their brains would be trying to come to terms with what they were witnessing. Quick control is key. This involved a great deal of shouting from the men, which commanded the staff's attention and compliance.

The gang wore identical boots, gloves, balaclavas and weapons, so it would have been incredibly difficult to identify any individual among the three threatening, shouting men. The staff witness statements would have been absolutely no help to the police.

This gear doesn't sound anything unusual as kit for a gang, but it's the detail that counts. For instance, the balaclavas were bought from motorbike shops. Back then, the helmets that bikers wore came with a silk head covering which covered the ears and chin, but not the face. We would stitch up the mouth section, leaving only the eyes visible. One particular brand had eye sockets that were bordered with bright red stitching. When people stare at someone's face wearing this style of mask, they cannot tell the colour of the eyes because they are distracted by the red borders. Silk balaclavas were definitely superior to woollen ones. Firstly, silk doesn't impair your hearing and, secondly, you can quickly snatch it off your head and conceal it in your fist which you cannot with a woollen balaclava.

The footwear was usually police-issue boots. They had a Dr. Marten type of sole, were mid-calf length and made of black non-reflective nylon. They were incredibly light weight and had added ankle protection that gave the flexibility to run without restriction.

The gloves we used were made of fine leather and thin, so you could feel everything you touched. By far the best were golfing gloves, but inevitably they are sold in singles, so getting a matching pair takes time. You cannot buy a left and right glove from the same golf outlet without possibly raising suspicion, so we would buy one glove from one club and then travel around the country visiting other clubs until we found the matching left or right to make the pair.

Outside the bank, one of the team would act as a look-out and blend in as an unseen civilian near the target area, just in case a warning had to be sent to those inside. All of those involved carried walkie-talkies and these would only be used if absolutely necessary.

Another gang member would be on a pedal bike cycling slowly around to observe and, if needed, block a road if anything untoward was spotted. Someone else would be in a car that would conveniently break down at an appointed time, allowing a quicker getaway once the gang left the bank.

From dropping through the ceiling to climbing

into the getaway car with hundreds of thousands, if not millions, of guilders took about three and a half minutes.

The driver of the hire car would focus purely on driving, while the person who sat in the passenger seat, who would have been one of the three robbing the bank, just shouted instructions and directions.

When you are driving safely, but at great speed, your attention needs simply to be on the driving and not thinking about where to turn, or if you are going in the right direction.

The pillion would make snap decisions and guide the driver. Meanwhile, in another rented car right behind there would be three gang members. A driver and a passenger in the front, and one behind perched in the middle of the back seats holding a pump-action shotgun. This was loaded with a stop bullet, not to cause any harm to people, but to slow down any police vehicles that might follow.

A stop bullet passing through the car radiator into the sump engine block will seriously slow anything down. Stop bullets were Netherlands police issue 9mm ammunition that were designed to enter a target and stay put. After impact, the green-tipped projectile splinters, blasting a crater where it hits, effectively immobilising anything with minimal collateral damage.

Believe me, you do not need to kill anyone if you

just want to get away with armed robbery.

Once inside the rental car, the men would strip off their overalls, balaclavas, bulletproof vests, boots, guns and ammunition, and put everything inside a large sports bag that was identical to the other bag which contained the stolen money.

The great thing about the guilder, which was the legal currency for Holland until the Euro was introduced in 2002, was that there were some notes minted in high value, so a wad of cash the thickness of a paperback book could amount to a hundred thousand guilders, or about ten thousand pounds.

At a completely isolated area, the gang would stop and replace the original number plates. This had to be done before a police helicopter could start to reconnoitre. The false plates were added to one of the bags.

Once a major offence has been committed, the police are all over the area like a rash. They form roadblocks several kilometres out of the town centre at such alarming speed that no car leaving the crime scene could drive quickly enough to avoid being caught at one of them. They are incredibly effective.

So, now dressed in civilian clothes, one of the gang would be dropped off near a railway station, taking both sports bags with him. He would buy a return ticket, and step onto the platform just as a train was pulling into the station. He would make sure the bags he carried didn't look heavy and certainly no one could tell what they contained as they were expertly packed.

This gang member would simply head home. He would be travelling away from the town, so against the rush-hour commute. This meant there were fewer people, and he would have enough room to sit down and keep the bags very close.

Unsurprisingly, all of the team were known to the police. But, regardless of how suspicious it looked when stopping three of them together in a hire car just minutes after a bank robbery, the police never found any grounds on which to make an arrest.

They were always cooperative with the police, allowing the car and themselves to be searched, but with absolutely no evidence, despite what the police suspected, they had to let them drive away.

Later that day, they would all meet at the house where the two sports bags had ended up and split the spoils equally between them.

CHAPTER TEN

Leon was always ready when his phone rang. He didn't actually say anything to Dom as he knew time was of the essence. He paged everyone and leapt into his car, picking up another gang member on his way.

Belgium has very different gun legislation to Holland. It is a lot tighter with punishment if you are caught with one or suspected of having one. Simply wearing a bulletproof vest or having a couple of bullets in your pocket is proof enough.

We reached Antwerp port in twenty minutes. The entrance gave us a great vantage point and we arrived just as the two trucks we needed to look out for were leaving the dockside. Obviously, we didn't know which one was being driven by Dom, or which one contained the hash.

The plan was to follow both. Having got back to the cars, we drove behind the trucks. It became apparent that they were going to travel in the same direction, rather than separate onto different routes. This made our life a whole heap easier.

Buck peeled off from us once we crossed back into Holland and he made his way back to the safe house to collect vests, guns and ammunition. We had walkie-talkies to communicate with and, although the maximum reach was only a couple of kilometres, we figured he would find us eventually.

I actually don't know how long Buck had been gone, but it couldn't have been more than twenty minutes. We took it in turns to pull off the motorway to equip ourselves. This also prevented us looking suspicious to the truck drivers. Having four cars between us made it easier to be less conspicuous but obviously we stayed within the range of our walkie-talkies.

The beauty of Holland is that it is a flat country. You really can see for miles, so we were able to keep track of the lorries from a safe distance of about a kilometre, even when they had left the motorway.

Knowing we hadn't been spotted, and acutely aware that we had to get possession as quickly as possible, we sped to the area where we had last seen the trucks disappear off the road. It happened to be a tiny village with about twenty houses and a small industrial unit, all of which was unfamiliar to us. By now we had been travelling for an hour and a half.

As we turned into the hamlet, we saw a white Mercedes and, sitting in the driver's seat was the man who was clearly there to give the new driver instructions about which warehouse to take the truck to. This driver had no idea what his cargo was, but he was instructed to check the trailers for tracking devices, just in case someone had slipped one into the back.

By the time we turned up, one of the trucks had had its trailer uncoupled. We pounced. With incredible speed and dexterity, Buck blew out the Mercedes' tyres while almost simultaneously leaping onto the bonnet and firing wildly for a few seconds. He then remained completely still as he aimed his assault rifle steadily at the driver's face through the windscreen a mere foot away.

All sorts of random things started to happen. Everyone seemed to be firing guns while the driver of the uncoupled trailer started to make a getaway in the cab. Two of our cars followed him. Then, to everyone's surprise, the cab suddenly turned back on itself and started chasing our cars. It was farcical. There was no sign of Dom. The saving grace was that it was nine o'clock at night, dark, and pretty quiet. If there were people around, no one had yet called the police.

The cat-and-dog chase seemed to fizzle out, with people scattering everywhere. It was the perfect chance to take the truck that had the trailer still attached. There were no keys, but with my past experience and knowledge of almost any vehicle, I was able to hot-wire it. It drove for two hundred meters and then the brakes locked. I was a good mechanic and was sure I could fix it.

I couldn't fix it.

We knew one man who could help. He was the most skilled car starter I had ever known and incredibly quick. He was a friend of Mick and, luckily, a creature of habit so I knew he was going to be in one of three brothels all within a fifteen-minute, hundred-mile-an-hour drive away.

He was found completely out of his head. He hadn't got a clue what was going on or why he was being driven at breakneck speed and being slapped around the face while having espressos poured down his throat.

The espressos had no effect whatsoever. My Dutch wasn't that great, but it was better than his English. I managed to explain that the brakes on a lorry had seized. As we pulled up there were two of the gang ready to pull Mick's friend from my car into the truck to get cracking.

I asked for a torch. No one had a torch. Could you believe it? We had enough hardware to win a war, and years of experience in crime and kidnapping. We could break into any building, safe, car, lorry or ship, and owned rolls of Semtex and hand grenades, but we did not have a torch between us. Geez.

For whatever reason, I shouted 'lumière', which

was the first word that came into my head. Lumière actually means light in French.

Our spaced-out new friend shouted 'vuur', thinking that's what I meant. Vuur is Dutch for fire. It sounded about right so I nodded in agreement, whereupon he whipped out a lighter and set light to the wires exposed under the dash. There must have been years of oil and grime on the wires because they went up like paper and, within seconds, the whole the cabin was on fire.

There was nothing we could do but stand back and watch it go up in smoke. The only advantage was that we had managed to move it two hundred meters and it was tucked up on a lane, pretty much out of sight from the main road.

I couldn't believe it. I had spent a year of my life driving Dom every weekend to warehouse locations owned by the company whose truck we had successfully just set light to, and there was nothing I could do about it.

Someone drove our drunk friend back to the brothel and we split into groups and made our way home, gutted that we had got so near, but were now so far from our goal.

Chapter Eleven

I had been living in a spare flat belonging to Chris for about a year. With the gang's increasing successes, it was getting harder to store things and especially any people we needed to kidnap. We had a meeting and decided to find a bigger place where we could stock pile weapons and ammunition as well as uniforms and accessories. Getting a safe house seemed like a plan.

We agreed that the costs would be split between us. It made sense that I would live at the premises, so Buck and I set about trying to find the ideal location.

By living at the premises, I would take responsibility for looking after all the paraphernalia.

It was obvious we needed a house with no neighbours, large storage facilities, near main roads, but in a quiet setting that was hard to locate. We soon realised this wasn't going to be an easy find, but we worked at it every single day. We scoured local papers, newsagents and notice boards. It took us over a month, but we found what seemed like the perfect place.

The property was a house. The owner had no family in the area, and he had to travel to America for work, for at least a year. It had a tiny basement area under the stairs which was big enough to stand up in and perfect for any kidnapees.

For decades it has been legal to smoke weed in Holland, with many cafés selling it on request to anyone popping in for a coffee. This makes hash quite a lucrative business, so many people simply grow it in their own homes. However, on a larger scale, it is better to rent a place and grow it in someone else's.

If I had turned up at an estate agency on my own, wearing a sharp suit with a gold Rolex and speaking Dutch, they would have immediately assumed I wanted the house to grow weed, and would not have leased it to me.

I needed to have a good back story for the estate agent or, as you might say, a respectable image. Luckily for me, Marjorie was married to one of the gang and she was asked to escort me to the agency, posing as my wife.

Marjorie was extremely prim and proper. She had short dark hair and, on the day of our prearranged appointment, she wore a modest skirt and woollen jacket. Think of *Mrs Doubtfire*. To be fair, this was her usual attire, so nothing out of the ordinary. She also happened to speak with a perfect English accent.

I wore a polo neck jumper, a Rupert Bear check jacket, smart trousers, hand-made leather brogues and I'd shaved my head. We were the archetypal middle-class British couple to look at.

The agent was fairly dodgy, so when I called to stipulate that I wanted to pay cash, he was more than willing to go along with it.

Marjorie and I walked in hand in hand, smiling and laughing. We explained that we had just got married and I was a writer looking to complete a novel. I would need at least a year and we wanted to be away from England, in relative peace and quiet, to enjoy our honeymoon period.

I was a complete pain to Marjorie. I kept pinching her bottom, kissing her on the cheek and generally being over touchy. She hated it and kept batting me away. This just made me worse. Most importantly, it was a complete distraction to the agent. He was getting caught up in our silliness and, as a result, we knew he wouldn't remember what we looked like, but would recall how we had behaved. He got quite red-faced with our antics at one point.

The house was perfect. Access to it was over a track and up a long drive. It had a huge garage, big enough to fit in several stolen cars. It also had a workshop. It was a seven-minute drive to the centre of town, close to the Belgian border, but in the heart of the countryside in a charming village.

In each room we entered we discussed what we could use it for, where our furniture would go, how lovely it would be when friends came for a weekend and where my writing desk could be situated. We chit-chatted in the garden and discussed which flowers would look good to enhance its beauty.

We made it clear to the agent that we were thrilled with the house and felt it suited our needs down to the ground.

Once back at the office, I reiterated that I was only prepared to pay cash. This clearly suited the agent, as he could take some off the top for himself. He was also more than happy when I said I didn't want any receipts or, in fact, anything in writing. With this tacit agreement, I paid a three-month deposit in cash, shook him by the hand, grabbed Marjorie in a place she did not want to be grabbed, and left.

Marjorie barracked me throughout the entire journey back to her house and gave me a couple of slaps as I reached across to squeeze her thigh. The more she told me off, the more I laughed. But I knew I couldn't have done it without her. She was the perfect cohort. Now I had a new home without there being any trace of me in the country.

Chapter Twelve

So, after an incredibly disappointing night, we were forced to walk away from a burning truck and potentially from hash that we didn't actually know existed. However, because there had been a scout in the white Mercedes waiting for the trucks, it seemed highly probable that there was hash in those containers.

Four of us ended up in Chris's flat where we discussed a wide range of possibilities. I had drunk so much coffee that I was beginning to shake and, in my frustration, I said that I had to go back to see if there was anything that could be done.

Verdun thought two heads were better than one and said he'd join me.

It was about six-thirty on a Sunday morning. We drove sedately so as not to draw attention to ourselves, because there was very little traffic around at that time of day.

We parked the car in amongst others about a quarter of a mile from where we left the trailer and didn't speak as the slip road came into view.

We could hear commotion, but couldn't quite see, so found a vantage point in a thicket of tall shrubs and watched as the local police unhitched the cab and hooked the trailer to a police tow truck. There was no sign of the other trailer and, given it had been several hours since we left the scene, we were keen to hang around to see where they took it.

We walked back to our car and, at a safe distance, followed the police. We kept at least two kilometres from them. Verdun knew the area well enough to guess where the truck was going. His hunch was right.

Once again, we parked the car away from the police station, walking through dykes so we couldn't be seen. At a safe distance we saw the police tow the entire trailer into a large warehouse.

The actual police station was on one side of a road which led to a small business unit with about six companies operating from it. The police warehouse was on the opposite side of the road, about fifty meters away. Because of the sloping landscape, it was lower than the police station, and tucked behind a dyke, so the only thing you could see from the station was the roof of the warehouse.

We had seen enough, so we followed our footsteps back to the car and, while I drove, Verdun sent a code to the gang which gave a time and place to meet.

We decided to go back later that day as Sundays are notoriously quiet and being a fairly provincial station, there was a reasonable chance there wouldn't be many police around either.

I desperately needed some sleep so headed to bed for a few hours. As I'd been so involved and invested so much time, the others felt it only fair that I go back with Verdun to suss out the warehouse and check the security around the building. I knew if anyone could break in, I was going to be with the best man in the country to do it.

Chapter Thirteen

Our success was largely down to information that was given to us. What we did with this information helped us to get rich but, equally, we always carefully thought through every aspect of any job we undertook.

One of our biggest strengths was our contacts. Between us we knew a lot of people and our reputation did go before us. If someone came to us with a problem and we could help out, then that was what we did.

We really appreciated nice cars, so it was a bit of a no-brainer when Leon had an approach from the owner of a top-end car showroom. Leon had his own garage that repaired and sold cars, so was known to many other dealers in the district.

The initial contact came from a man who had been swindled out of six cars. He was no fool, so the person who had pulled this off must have been one hell of a con man.

It had started about three years earlier when a man entered his dealership looking to buy high-end cars for some of his clients. He was a bit of a fixer for wealthy people who didn't have the time to go and purchase things themselves. He was charming, likeable and had a limitless budget.

The dealership happened to be just over the border in Belgium where the con lived and, on his first visit, he bought a Ferrari with cash.

He bought a Porsche on his second visit a month later, again paying in cash.

A few months in, he bought two cars at one time. He had a friend with him to drive the second car, but only paid for one, promising he would return the following day and pay for the second. He was absolutely true to his word and returned the next day to make the payment.

The dealer had done his due diligence and researched this high-powered, vastly lucrative man. He found a very professional webpage with photographs of him alongside his rich and famous clients. So, after he had known this buyer for over a year, he continued to allow him to take a car away without paying immediately, on the promise that the payment would be quickly made. It always was.

One month the buyer took three cars and paid for two, saying he would return two days later to pay for the third. As usual, good to his word, that's exactly what happened.

In the event the buyer requested cars that were

not in stock, the dealer would source them and call the con to view them once they were in the showroom. So, a good bond had developed, and the dealer actually started to consider this rich new client as a friend.

Initially, the dealer had been a bit unnerved, but now taking a car with only the promise of paying for it, was becoming more regular. He had earned really good money over the eighteen months the con had been coming to his dealership so, weighing all things up, he was too good to let go.

After a couple of years, the client still bought cars, but and the period between taking them and paying for them was lengthening. In fact he possessed several cars he had yet to pay for.

One day he stopped coming altogether and the dealer couldn't reach him through any of his known contacts. With each car he had handed over the service history, log books and the spare car keys and he was now out of pocket for five of them.

The build-up of trust over nearly three years had worked like a charm and he felt a complete fool for falling for this scam. It was at this point he made a call to Leon.

Having heard this sob story from Leon, one of us checked out the dealership to find that it was a legitimate business in Belgium, all above board and taxes paid. Given this information, we figured the dealer could claim the insurance for his lost cars. He knew where the con lived, so we reckoned if he couldn't face the con himself to get his gear back, then he sure as hell wouldn't have the guts to face us.

In our experience, the type of man who carries out this sort of con tends to rely on the gift of the gab to achieve his goals. It was highly likely that he didn't feel the need to carry, or even own, a firearm. He would feel confident that he could talk his way out of any situation. In fact, he wouldn't really see himself as a criminal, as no one actually gets hurt in these circumstances, except perhaps the insurance companies.

We needed to be absolutely sure that our con was going to be home, so we hatched a plan and decided to drop in on him one Friday evening. It just so happened it was December twenty-fourth. We wore smart casual clothes with stab vests underneath and rang the doorbell. As soon as he opened the door, we walked past him straight into his kitchen/dining room, where we found a young couple sitting at the dining table eating a meal.

The strangest thing was they just carried on eating, without the slightest interest in us or their host, who was being ushered into a seat. One of us stood next to him, ensuring there was nothing close by that he could use as a weapon.

The rest of us went through his entire house collecting the paperwork and keys for the 'stolen' cars, two of which were conveniently parked outside his house.

During the search we also found cash, Rolex watches, jewellery and other useful items to sell. We also removed the watch from his wrist and took a key for a lock-up he owned in Rotterdam, which was only about a twenty-minute drive away.

It was clear the items we took had been a result of other scams and, as we had no conscience, we took the lot.

Two of the gang raced off in the Ferraris, both 328 GTS, one red, one black, while the rest of us headed off to the lock-up. At his warehouse we discovered a Peugeot 605 3 Litre SV24, three Mercedes, a Maserati, and a couple of jet skis.

Even though we didn't expect this to be a difficult job, we had still planned it down to the last detail. However, Chris had decided to take a couple of lines of coke and had got into his head that it would be a good idea to take this whole adventure a little further.

There was no point in arguing with him, unless you fancied being shot, so four of us piled into a car with the con sitting in between Chris and Verdun on the back seat.

We drove fifty kilometres to a police station in

Wuustwezel, Belgium, which, by unlucky coincidence, is where I had rented a house and where my wife and two children were presently living, waiting for me to get home to share Christmas dinner. This took place a few months before we got a safe house.

As you would expect on Christmas Eve, there was very little traffic on the roads, and I suspected I had a very pissed-off wife at home.

I can only guess that Chris thought that because the dealership was in Belgium, the dealer would have reported his loss to the local coppers. So, this being the nearest police station to the dealership, was where we ended up. It was tiny and, given the time of day, we were surprised that it was actually manned.

I was driving, so I parked the car opposite the police station while Chris got out, dragging the con with him. Chris was carrying a Glock in his waistband.

We watched as he entered, thinking there might be a bit of trouble, and then sat around for half an hour. This was a really long time to be waiting outside a police station on Christmas Eve so, not sure what else to do and with absolutely no sign of Chris, I started to drive away, doing about thirty kilometres an hour.

Bear in mind we were loitering and carrying guns

in a country that could be politely described as a banana republic, as their policy was to shoot first and ask questions later.

By now it was about ten at night and the roads were completely deserted. Within five minutes of moving off, a police car raced up behind us. Verdun screamed for me to put my foot down and scram, but logic kicked in.

There were three of us and only one of him so, even though this could have gone horribly wrong, I pulled over and wound the window down. Before I could say anything, the copper asked us if we were the friends of the debt collector back at the nick. When I confirmed that we were, he asked me to follow him back to the station as our colleague was ready for collection.

As casual as you like, Chris strolled out of the police station, over the road and got into the back of the car as if he hadn't a care in the world.

It transpired that he had entered the station, explained to the copper on duty that the man he was holding was wanted in Belgium for fraud. He had simply stated that he was a debt collector, working for an agency in Holland. He was bolshie and confident to the point where he was not asked for, and did not produce, any ID to back this up.

Chris actually walked the con through to the custody suite, with a gun down his waistband and totally out of his head on coke. They arrested the con even though he wasn't a wanted man, and he spent the night in the cells. However, as there was no evidence against him, the police had to release him on Christmas morning.

A couple of days later, having had fun running around in the cars, we took them to our usual contact who owned a legitimate car dealership twenty-seven kilometres southeast of Rotterdam. He was a friend of Mick's dad and we nicknamed him Pig, because the translation of his surname into English was bacon.

Pig had a good business and knew his way around cars, but he was no fool, and understood exactly who we were and how we had probably come across these beautiful vehicles. He wouldn't touch any car unless it had all the supporting paperwork. Luckily, almost all of the weasels we took cars from tended to be very meticulous in keeping log books, service history and spare keys.

He bought all the cars except the Peugeot, as I'd taken a bit of a shine to it. So, Pig bent the rules, turned a blind eye and drove a hard bargain. There wasn't a great deal of negotiation either, but he was usually more than fair, because he didn't want to lose this source of easy income.

Obviously, there was a little quid pro quo going on, in as much as we would pay the listed price for a car we wanted from Pig's showroom in cash. This money would go straight into his back pocket under the proviso that the car remained listed as being owned by his business. That way, if any of us got stopped by the police for some ridiculous misdemeanour, they couldn't actually take the car away because the legitimate owner was Pig's business.

Whenever we came across any jewellery or watches that we needed to sell, we usually went through Mick's dad. His nickname was Pavarotti, for no other reason than he was the absolute spit of him and, like Pig, he was no pushover. Again, he wouldn't buy any watch unless it had certificates, paperwork, and boxes to endorse the product. Luckily, that was invariably how we found them, which was handy.

Chapter Fourteen

I woke feeling better, not just because I had needed the sleep, but because I felt there had to be more to the trailer and its contents, as the police had made the effort to drive it to their warehouse.

It was late afternoon when Verdun and I drove back to the police station. Again, we parked about a quarter of a mile away and the dyke we walked through ran past the warehouse. The door was facing out over a field and, as luck had it, was not on the side nearest to the police station.

We stood for a while looking and listening for anything. We needed to check that there weren't patrol guards or anything that might trigger attention in the police station. Once completely satisfied that we were on our own, we scrambled up the dyke to the huge roller shutter. Obviously, this would make noise if we attempted to enter through it, but about twenty meters to our right was single fire escape door.

Verdun, being an expert burglar, carried with him

an array of tools which gave him the ability to break into anything, including cars, safes, and buildings and, as it turned out, police warehouses.

We both took a long hard look at the structure. Verdun blinked a couple of times in slight disbelief, then turned towards me smiling and said:

'It's made of wood.'

He grabbed a plaster saw and started cutting a hole big enough to get his head through, being careful not to trigger any alarm system. Without further ado, he slowly stuck his head inside.

'It didn't click.'

'What do you mean, it didn't click?'

'Just that, and there's no cameras either.'

He enlarged the hole so it was big enough to climb inside and replaced the piece of wood. He then opened the fire escape door, grinning like a fool.

The warehouse was enormous, at least seventy meters long by fifty meters wide. At the far end, furthest from the door, was the now-empty trailer. There were thousands of five-kilogram tins of apricots, divided into two piles on the floor next to it.

We ran over and grabbed a tin from each side and shook it. Verdun clearly had a tin of fruit, whereas the one I was shaking emitted a dull thud. Realising what we had our hands on, we contacted Leon and told him we needed transport.

We did a rough calculation and reckoned we would need five or six long-wheel-based transit vans.

The key to pulling anything off, especially when your proximity to the police is so close, is to make everything look normal. So there would be no point in having ten vans when five would do.

The police station was situated on a minor road which gave access to an industrial unit where vans formed the usual flow of traffic that went past.

We were meticulous in ensuring the vans weren't overloaded either. The last thing you want is for the cops to pull you over because the vehicle looks too heavy. You also don't want to get stopped for stupid things, like not wearing a seat belt. So, although there was a sense of urgency, doing stupid things at this stage wouldn't get us anywhere.

Getting the vans took a little while.

Over the years that we had been working together, we had made a mental note of vehicles that might end up being of some use to us. As it happened, the vans we needed were a popular choice with self-employed builders.

The law in Holland dictated that the vehicle only needed to be insured and not the individual so, as long as it was legal and roadworthy, then anyone with a valid licence could drive it.

Leon was one of five of the gang who went out on the hunt for vans, but they all had a pretty good idea where to look and knew that time was of the essence. Being a Sunday evening, many of the painters and decorators were at home with their vans parked outside.

Leon's approach was typical of any of the team. The van owner, once at the door, would be greeted with a smile and a polite introduction. Leon would ask if he could borrow the van for twenty-four hours and, in exchange for the owner's co-operation, he would pay one hundred thousand guilders, or about a thousand pounds. This was equivalent to about a month's wage, so invariably the van owner would be delighted to help.

The pair would empty the contents of the van somewhere out of sight and then Leon would be handed the keys. It takes an element of skill to convince someone to part with their vehicle for a day, given it would be worth more than our borrowing fee. I do suspect some of the people knew who we were and wouldn't have dared refuse our request for help.

Knowing it would take them a while to reach us, Verdun and I started the painful task of carrying what ended up being 1,666 cans across the length of the warehouse. By the time Leon turned up with the first van, I reckon we had moved a quarter of the cans.

The rest of the gang communicated with walkie-talkies, so only one van turned up at a time.

The only access to the warehouse was past the police station and, once again, we had luck on our side. The reception area either wasn't occupied, or the police had their backs to the window, so they didn't notice the traffic activity which would have been unusual for a Sunday evening.

So, the three of us carefully, but quickly, loaded the van so that the tins were balanced and wouldn't shift around. It was packed to its weight capacity and not a kilo over. Leon then drove the load to a middle-of-the-road hotel about thirty kilometres away, just off the motorway. It was back-breaking carrying so many tins across the warehouse but, as incentives go, it was right up there. Before I left in the last van, I shook all the remaining cans to ensure that the police hadn't inadvertently missed any. They hadn't, which was extremely thoughtful of them.

As it happened, I was in the passenger seat, which was closest to the police station and, by coincidence, as we passed, a policeman happened to be looking out the window so, without hesitation, I gave a little wave as we departed. To my delight he waved back.

We had packed five vans in total and parked them

next to each other at the hotel. We paid cash for our lodgings and ensured we had rooms that overlooked the car park, not that anyone was likely to take our vehicles.

The reason we didn't drive the vans immediately to the lock-up Leon had sorted out for us, was because it is unusual for work transit vans to be seen on a motorway after dark on a Sunday evening. It's the same with heavy plant vehicles, they are never moved at night.

Aside from that, it is hard to chase someone in rush hour traffic, so we would be completely inconspicuous at eight on a Monday morning on a busy slow-moving motorway.

The following day we all ate a hearty breakfast and drove the further fifteen kilometres to what would be our home for the next three days.

The lock-up belonged to a friend of Leon, called Pieter, who owed him a favour. It had a toilet and small kitchenette area and was big enough to get the vans inside and close the shutter so no one could see us.

As each van was unloaded it was pressure washed, then driven by the same gang member who borrowed it to a garage near the home of its owner where it was refuelled. It was returned with no questions asked and absolutely no evidence as to what it might have transported.

Mick was the first man back and he had been tasked to buy some tin openers. What a twit. We had 1,666 five-litre catering tins, and he had bought cheap old-fashioned stab can openers, the ones with a corkscrew attachment.

Chris grabbed one and opened the first tin. Inside was a two-kilo disc of lead wrapped in newspaper with three kilos of top-end pure hash.

We had just stolen five tons of hash from the local police station. We knew it was highly unlikely that this would make big headlines. However, it became a well-known story throughout the criminal fraternity that we had pulled it off.

I would love to have seen the faces of various people on Monday morning. Not only of the police when they discovered their haul was now only tins of apricots, but also the bloke in the white Mercedes who had been arrested for importing the hash, when he was told he was free to leave, because the evidence against him had disappeared in the night.

Chapter Fifteen

Successful rip deals not only rely on planning, detail and a little bit of luck, but they also work when people believe what they are seeing. In order to see a deal through, you need to create a situation to lure someone to the bait without causing any alarm, as you lead up to their capture.

Mick was enjoying an espresso and reading a paper at a bar in town when he received a tip that one of the local café owners was going to come into a large quantity of hash to sell to some of his more discerning customers. Oddly, this was a café none of us visited as a rule, not because we didn't like the gay man who owned it, but because Leon couldn't stand gay men.

We all had our own opinions as to why Leon was so anti but decided never to mention them to his face. Behind his back was fine though.

So our target was a man called Tim who owned a couple of bars locally and lived with his Indonesian boyfriend. After further questioning of the tipster, we discovered the hash haul was due to arrive in the next couple of days. This was great as it actually gave us more time to plan than we thought.

We supplied many cafés throughout our patch and were, I have to admit, a tad pissed off that Tim had never made an approach to us to acquire some for him.

We knew he did a few hash deals throughout the year, but nothing outstanding. Although he was on our patch, he didn't really come into our radar sights as the quantities of hash he bought generally weren't worth us getting out of bed for.

Given Leon's general hatred of Tim and the quantity of hash expected, we decided it might be a nice idea to make a house call.

So we found where he lived and plotted the best place to capture him.

The area we had chosen was very close to his home and, having done a recce of the place, we ensured that there were enough of us to block every possible exit. This was in case Tim or his boyfriend suddenly tried to make a run for it.

At the time we didn't have the safe house, so the plan was to kidnap Tim and take him to Leon's garage. It was a business that had a forecourt full of cars, a workshop for repairs, and an office where his wife often worked. It was open six days a week with a full complement of staff.

A couple of days later word got to us that Tim was in receipt of the hash, although at this point we didn't know how much, or where it was being stored. There was no time like the present, so we planned our attack to take place that evening.

Tim and his boyfriend had gone out to dinner that night, and afterwards they went on to a popular gay nightclub. One of the gang members had closely followed them to the club while another was already inside to check nothing untoward happened to the pair, who left in one piece having enjoyed a marvellous evening.

We got the code to say they had left the club at about one in the morning, bearing in mind that it was a school night, and Chris had two cafés to prepare and open the next day.

Leon and Verdun waited about a kilometre up the road, knowing Tim would have to pass them to get home. As he drove past, they casually pulled in behind him, leaving a big enough gap to look as though they were not following, but close enough to ensure nothing got in between the two cars.

Chris and I were already in position at the appointed place where we intended to inconvenience them. From the nightclub to where the ambush was going to take place was about six kilometres, and we were no more than a couple of hundred meters from Tim's front door.

The drive into his complex was one way and, as you rounded a corner into the estate, there were parked cars to the left, and a two-foot-high wall to the right. There were beautiful flower beds bordering a pristine lawn with mature trees, all of which were used as a communal space for the occupants of this expensive development.

Once you were committed to this section of road, there was no possible way to negotiate your way out of it as you were effectively hemmed in on both sides.

Tipp was sitting in a Mercedes sedan which he had parked earlier in the day. He was probably one of the dullest men I have ever had the displeasure to meet. He spoke in a drawl about absolutely nothing. I reckon there was a greater chance of anyone we kidnapped being bored to death by him than by any mental torture we could inflict on them.

He was useful to the gang as an outsider because he knew Rotterdam like the back of his hand and, no matter how obscure the contact we might need for a job, he could always get hold of the person we wanted.

Tipp was dressed in a pair of crumpled trousers, wearing old, scuffed shoes, and a hand-knitted jumper that his gran had badly sewn together a couple of Christmases ago. He had slightly unkempt hair and had donned a pair of spectacles with lightly tinted lenses which were so thick his eyes looked twice their actual size.

Tim and his boyfriend were now half a kilometre away, with Leon and Verdun still at a reasonable distance in the car behind, still far enough away not to be noticed.

As they turned the corner into the complex, Tipp, who was eighty meters away, started to attempt to reverse the long Mercedes out of his parking spot. He was making a right balls-up of it. On the first attempt he hit the kerb, so he drove back into the spot and tried again. He cranked the gears and got halfway out which forced Tim to slow. Then Tipp made a bit more of an effort, but by now he had got stuck too far out for Tim and his boyfriend to pass.

Tipp lent backwards, waving his arm in an apologetic way, while cranking the gears again and now looking agitated as he was clearly holding someone up.

Tim's car came to a halt while the debacle unfolded in front of him.

Back then, when cars came to a complete stop, the doors automatically unlocked.

Tim was so distracted, by what looked like a complete idiot who was clearly unable to reverse, he didn't notice that Leon and Verdun had slowly and silently drawn up behind them, less than six inches from their boot.

Chris and I ran from opposite sides of the road angling ourselves so we couldn't be seen in Tim's wing mirrors. Within seconds, and simultaneously, we wrenched the passenger and driver doors open, pulling the startled men from their car. Tipp jumped out and opened the boot of his Mercedes, while Chris threw Tim in the back and I threw his squeaking boyfriend into the boot of Leon's car.

I drove Tim's car to his house and parked it in his usual place, taking his keys with me, and then jumped back in beside Chris and we made our way to Leon's garage.

The whole kidnap ordeal had taken thirty seconds and had gone like clockwork. Tim was already tied with thick straps to a plastic garden chair when we turned up eight minutes later.

Leon hated Tim so much he had asked if he could conduct the questioning and any necessary torture he felt would help. We agreed to this under the condition he didn't do anything stupid, and he got the point, so we could get on with finding and stealing the hash.

The reason we used plastic garden chairs was because they were easy to wash down after a kidnapping where bodily fluids might have been extracted. Not by our tortures, but because these fluids tended to leave the body when someone was shit-scared about what was going to happen to him.

Leon started the quizzing but, unfortunately, he was dealing with a bright man and, half an hour in, Tim had spoken a lot but said absolutely nothing. He'd been slapped about a bit, but Leon was getting nowhere.

At that point he decided to clamp Tim's testicles and apply some volts to see if that moved things along a bit. After all, Leon had experienced this treatment when he had been kidnapped by Spic and Span, so why not give it a go. Luckily, I looked across just as he was connecting the amp, not the volts, from a commercial battery.

Amps will kill you, volts won't. In the event you want to build an electric fence to keep cattle in, you only need enough power to give them a tingle and a bit of a shock, so one amp should do the trick. Leon was about to zip thirteen amps through Tim's testicles. I reckoned at the very least it would leave burn marks and cause a great deal of pain and, at worst and most likely, it would kill him. This was not how we operated, so I stepped in and took over.

Apart from Leon and Tim, no one else in the room spoke. We all knew what we needed to do, so the less said the better.

What Leon needed to do, was get a bloody move on.

He had a garage that was going to open in the

morning, and Tim had cafés to run which meant he would be missed if he didn't turn up. We couldn't afford for anyone to raise an alarm or call the police.

So with Leon pissing about and getting nowhere, I decided to take matters into my own hands. It didn't take much, I stopped Leon in his amp tracks, then simply strolled into the adjacent room, grabbed Tim's boyfriend, marched him in, and started tying him to a chair. We would never kidnap a man's female partner, as much as anything because it averted the paranoia of being paid back in kind. But, in this instance, his boyfriend was fair game. Halfway through, it was clear Tim realised that I had taken the power from him, as I was strapping the love of his life to a chair, and it was obvious I was prepared to hurt him.

Tim started to talk.

That's all it took and he sang like a canary.

His house keys were on the same keyring as his car key and, once we knew where the hash was, a few of the gang dashed back to search his place. We took everything useful to us, including personal details like business contacts and national insurance numbers.

Sadly, we didn't get as much as we were expecting. In the end it was about five million guilder or about fifty thousand pounds, but that wasn't the point of the exercise. We wanted to teach him a lesson for dealing in hash without having previously involved us, and to shake him up a bit. He faded into the background after this incident and we never heard anything again about him or his boyfriend.

Chapter Sixteen

The deal Leon had done with Pieter to secure the lock-up was that we could use it for a week in return for the lead and scrap metal.

After we left the place, Pieter was instructed that he had less than twenty-four hours to clear the place up.

Once you were committed to working together, that is exactly what you did until you saw the job through. Sometimes we were gone from home days at a time, and sometimes weeks. It was just the way it went and none of us thought anything of it.

With all the cans unloaded and the vans returned to their rightful owners, eight of us sat down to the task in hand. We were cursing Mick with great vehemence because, by the time we'd each opened our third can, our hands were bleeding profusely. The tin openers were shredding our fingers, and the more we bled the more profuse our language became.

So we worked together, only leaving the

warehouse to get food. The first one who felt hungry got the job. We didn't get just any old takeaway crap, but really good wholesome deli food: salmon, pâté and things that we could see behind a glass plate, not stuff viewed from a photograph above a counter.

It made sense that the person picking up lunch also bought sports bags. The slight difficulty was that we needed at least two hundred of them, and it is surprisingly hard to get hold of nondescript bags in such quantities.

In the three days that we worked together, only Moon left for what he described as a domestic issue. His personal mobile phone rang, which wasn't the best of things, as anything that could trace us to a time and place in the middle of a heist was a complete no-no.

Ironically, Moon was an ex-copper who had been fully trained in the Dutch police as part of the arresting team. In Holland they had police who only went out to arrest people, and he was responsible for providing the gang with uniforms and stop bullets.

Moon was incredibly supple and athletic. Probably the best way to describe him would be as a young Hannibal Lecter. He also had a history of robbing banks. Once he had selected a bank, and after some careful observation, he would walk in equipped with a balaclava, a tracksuit, and an Uzi, and then walk out with a bag of money.

His getaway was the real coup de grace: under his tracksuit he wore a three-piece suit and switched his running shoes for leather-soled wingtips, then slid inside his dad's Porsche 928 turbo, parked close by. The police never suspected him as he drove, in his sharp suit, through their roadblock for the robbery he had just committed, as he didn't match the profile of the robber.

The domestic issue transpired to be that Moon's wife wanted him home to babysit their child as she had a clay modelling class to attend.

He had been gone for over two hours, while we remained opening cans and bleeding. Mick was not a man to get on the wrong side of, believe me. I have seen him ticked off and it's not a pretty sight. He made the call to Moon to politely enquire what was taking so long, strongly suggesting that he got his derrière back to the warehouse before he had finished counting to three.

Oddly, Moon arrived before Mick had hung up. No one else left for anything other than food and bags until the job was complete.

The hash blocks were wrapped in a plastic similar to cellophane and then well-bound in brown packing tape. I mean masses of the stuff wrapped around in all directions. The better packed the hash usually meant the better the quality of the product.

We clearly couldn't keep the stash at the lock-up so, as soon as a couple of sports bags were filled, usually around twenty-five kilos a bag, the person getting lunch would hide them at different storage places around the area.

With each block being so well-wrapped it didn't emit an aroma, so we weren't concerned about anyone sniffing us out. It would have been a different story if we'd kept all five tons of it in one room, so the quicker we got it shifted the better.

Three days later, we had unpacked and distributed five tons of hash around our town. We were bleeding, dying for a shower and a sleep in a bed, but we had just taken hash worth 2,500,000,000 guilders, the equivalent of twenty-five million pounds from under the noses of the police, and nothing feels better than that.

Chapter Seventeen

When you are part of a gang, especially when you have spent years building a reputation, people either want to be part of it, or they think they are big enough to take you on and try to take over your territory.

Let's be clear, we were not the cast of *Ocean's Eleven*, we were a fearless fighting force and a group to be afraid of.

We had a reputation of being harsh but fair. We needed people to have the confidence to approach us with tips because, without a grass, we might not hear about anything going down in our patch. With our growing notoriety, people would seek us out to do jobs for them.

Leon was short. The rest of the gang stood at six-foot and over, so at five foot six I'm sure he felt the need to prove himself on occasions. He was unaware of the true meaning of the nickname we had given him. Obviously, we never mentioned it to his face and Leon genuinely believed that 'retard' meant 'retired and successful'.

Often Leon would be the one to deliver weed to café owners. A few weeks earlier he had dropped off twenty kilos to a man we nicknamed Beard simply because he had the most enormous, short, thick luxurious beard we had ever seen.

Beard had taken one look at Leon and decided he was a pushover, so, when he turned up a week after he had delivered the hash and asked for his money, Beard refused to pay him, with some excuse or another. Leon went on his way and a couple of days later he returned to be met with the same rebuttal. Having been polite and got nowhere, Leon decided to call a meeting with the rest of us, to resolve the situation.

What the Beard didn't fully grasp was that if you disrespect one of the gang you are, in effect, disrespecting all of the gang. I mean, we had a reputation to uphold, and we sure as hell were not going to let some slime ball, albeit a very big and strong slime ball, get away with it.

So, having monitored the Beard's café for a couple of days, we decided to pay him a visit.

Two of the group had entered his café separately about twenty minutes apart. One sat on a stool at the counter, while another tucked himself by the window. They blended in, drinking coffee, reading a paper, or on the phone. They looked like every other customer in the shop, so they were completely unnoticeable.

I liked to be first one into a building in these circumstances as it is vital to get control of the situation very quickly. It is a shock when so many people storm in shouting the odds. Four of us entered and our first task was to isolate Beard. His henchmen who ran forward to help him were quickly immobilised by the rest of the gang.

Beard was dragged into a back room, out of sight of the café, while civilians scattered and left. It was bedlam, but well organised bedlam, as all of us knew exactly what we had to do. Chris had taken on Beard by holding him up against a wall and using the butt of his gun to brutally remove his teeth.

It was incredibly effective and very bloody. I had just thrown a punch rendering one of Beard's men unconscious. In this situation you are not there for a fight like you might see in a film. You need to save your time and energy and deck someone with your first punch, putting all your power and energy into it so your opponent cannot hit you back.

Chris called my name, so I cleared the bar in one jump, heading towards him. Despite Chris obviously having control of the situation, he told me that Beard didn't seem to be frightened enough and asked me what I would recommend.

Luckily, I had just the thing in the form of a small hand grenade, which fitted perfectly into his mouth.

I'll grant you it took a bit of forcing, but his new look, with no teeth, helped tremendously.

I don't think I have ever seen a man's eyes go so wide so quickly as he started gasping for air through his bloody and caked nostrils.

With that I then dashed back to the far end of the bar, about thirty feet away, and managed a running kick to the face of Beard's right-hand man. It was a spectacular smash as I had speed and forward momentum on my side. I launched a perfect kick to his face and teeth went everywhere. The sheer force of my hobnail-booted delivery meant his jaw was clearly going to need several operations to get it back to normal.

Six of us stood silently as we watched grown men who thought they could take over our patch, insult us, not pay their dues and disrespect us, occasionally moan in pain, but mostly they were unconscious.

We had shown other gangs in the region that we would use extreme violence to maintain our status and that we weren't afraid of anyone.

We split up and quickly, but efficiently, scoured the place for cash and hash, taking anything else we thought might be useful and clearly not Beard's personal property.

We had upheld our reputation and proved our point in under six minutes.

Chapter Eighteen

The reason we only tended to deal in hash and never got involved with Class A drugs was because the latter were a lot more complicated and the risks were far greater, especially if you were thinking of exporting the stuff. But once we got a tip that hash was being imported into Holland or Belgium by another organised gang, we would make a plan to intercept it.

The one thing we could totally rely on was each other. We trusted everyone in our group. When we did a job, we got on with it. We rarely spoke because we were so well organised and each of us knew exactly what part he played in the plan.

When all of the hash was out of the lock-up we took time and care to clean the place up with bleach. The only evidence left behind were the cans, newspaper and lead.

Given the enormity of the theft and the acute embarrassment to the police, we needed to ensure that even the smallest details were dealt with to reduce the chances of being caught. Despite all the suspicions in the world, if there is no evidence to prove you did the job, they cannot make an arrest.

Leon did his due diligence and returned to the lock-up to meet Pieter twenty-four hours after we'd packed up and cleaned out. To his horror, nothing had been touched.

Pieter was just about to be defriended, in an extremely painful way.

Behind closed doors, and out of earshot to adjacent warehouses, Leon spelt out his future if the cans, lead and paper weren't dealt with immediately. Not that he needed a threat, but Leon gave the assurance that a couple of the gang would pop around in an hour to double check. They did, and he had.

Pieter clearly understood the trouble he was facing by not sorting out our waste. When two of the gang turned up an hour later, the place was spotless. It transpired he had removed the paper from the tins and burnt the lot along with the newspaper that covered the lead. Each tin was crushed and disposed of across numerous scrapyards over several months, so as not to raise suspicion. We never heard where the lead ended up.

Chapter Nineteen

Unless we were dealing with an aggressive competitor or kidnapee we did not use violence. Let's face it, the moment someone outside the gang, especially a member of the public, got hurt, the police would be after you. It might take them weeks, months or years, but they would always have something to dangle over your head like the sword of Damocles.

So it came as a bit of a surprise to hear from George Henshaw or, as he was more commonly known, Mr Ecstasy of Holland. If you had half a brain, you didn't cross him, or piss him off under any circumstances, but most especially if you were employed by him.

Like most powerful people who have worked hard to reach the top, he was highly respected throughout the underworld across Holland. George made a call to Leon and explained he had heard a rumour that the chemists making his pills had done something underhand. I don't know exactly what they had done but 'underhand' could be something as small as stealing ten guilders, all the way to making and selling ecstasy behind George's back. This was not how you behaved if you want to keep your safe and secure well-paid job, let alone remain alive.

George's right hand man was called Carl and his job, amongst other things, was to be the main communication link between the chemists and his boss.

After a fairly brief conversation with Leon, where George expressed his intense displeasure about what was going on, he asked us to get rid of the employees in any way we saw fit. The deal was that, in return for making them disappear, we could keep whatever we found at the laboratory. We could have the pills, the chemicals, and also the machinery used to make them.

A few days later, Carl provided the information on both chemists, including names and home addresses, with their family details. Both men were married with children. He also gave us the address of the lab and provided the place, time and date that he had arranged to meet the chemists and said he would leave the rest to us.

This was the easiest job we'd ever undertaken. George Henshaw wanted these snakes to learn a lesson, to the extent that their means of earning a living and their reputations were destroyed. He was so pissed off, he had told Leon he actually didn't want them to ever have the opportunity to work as chemists across the whole of Holland again.

God knows what they had done, but all we cared about was that we had George's complete support, and that Carl could be called on if we thought we needed any other specific details before we set about picking them up.

Carl arranged to meet the chemists in a café, and he deliberately sat so he was clearly visible from the doorway. However, to save unnecessary fuss and palaver, we grabbed them before they stepped over the threshold.

The men were immediately separated and taken away in two cars. I was driving one of them. Both men were in their early thirties and, although I can only speak for one of them, they seemed like very amiable people, certainly not the sort of men who would be foolish enough to get into the pickle they now found themselves in.

There was a total of five of us in my car and our kidnapped man sat uncomfortably between two of the gang in the back seat.

The address of the farmhouse where they were based was in the far north of Holland, well out of our patch, and it took a good two-hour drive to reach it.

On arrival, we took everything that could be

useful to us, including over a million pills that they had just finished manufacturing and thoughtfully packed into large sports bags. The ecstasy machine was too heavy to transport, so one of the team from the other car arranged a hire van with a tailgate suitable to take its weight. He planned to return later that day to collect it along with the cement mixer.

We crammed as much as we possibly could into my car which was a 500E Mercedes Brabus. The ecstasy-filled sports bags were placed in the boot and those that couldn't fit were put in the foot wells and on people's laps, including mine and the chemist. With all this weight the car was on its axles, but slowly and steadily we headed back to the safe house.

There were more pills left at the farmhouse but we had managed to take 1.2 million of them in one hit. Although my car was obviously overweight and therefore at risk of being stopped by the police, it was a chance I had to take. If someone else had found the farmhouse, or the police had been called because of the unusual activity, we would have had to abandon the lot, so it was vital to take as much as we could carry in the first hit.

Having been on the road for several hours, I suddenly felt hungry. We were about five kilometres from the safe house so I suggested picking up a McDonalds, which everyone agreed to.

Being the charming bunch of blokes we were, it felt only proper to get our kidnapped chemist to place the order. We pulled into the McDonalds drive-through and made him clearly state what we wanted, deliberately ordering a different meal for each one of us, along with assorted drinks and sauces. The chemist was told to only order four meals, so nothing for him. Mind you, after spending several very uncomfortable hours in our company, I doubt if he could have swallowed anything.

I paid cash and we ate as we drove the short distance back to the safe house. At this point we put a hood over the chemist's head as he was staying with us. His partner was released to go home and collect all the money they had made out of George. Not just spare cash, but all forms of identification, which included national insurance numbers, driving licence, social security cards, passports, address and note books, and any recent family pictures.

He went to his partner's house and did the same there. He was quick and compliant, so when we had photocopied this information, we agreed between us to give the originals back, once the men were finally released.

CHAPTER TWENTY

We took all this information from everyone we captured as it was vital to know everything about the people you are dealing with. You cannot afford to be surprised. It gives you a great advantage as it really fucks with people's heads if they think their family are at risk. However, if the kidnapee was a complete shit, difficult, uncooperative, or just a total wanker, we would take his personal information and not bother to return it.

We weren't in the habit of kidnapping for kidnapping's sake, but it was the fastest way to get information from people. Being taken against your will by a bunch of no-nonsense men is complete mental torture. No matter what Hollywood movies make you believe, there are no heroes holding out, waiting for the cavalry to arrive in the nick of time. Everyone talked.

People wanted to get out and away from us as quickly as possible. Preparation was key, but also a huge luxury as most targets were unpredictable, so we had to take advantage when the opportunity presented itself.

There were many considerations to bear in mind, such as how long you could keep people before they were likely to be missed, or if they depended on certain medications, or were diabetic. I mean we didn't want them to die on our watch, and especially not to die before they had imparted the information we needed from them.

No two kidnappings were the same. People, circumstances and information that we needed were different on each occasion. We might have got intelligence that only gave so much detail. The informer may have known that a consignment of hash was due into the country, the container it was in and the location of the warehouse, but not when it was going to arrive.

However, it was often highly probable that the informer could identify the man who was likely to know this final, vital part.

So, we would find out where this person lived, and establish his daily habits. What time he left for work, the route he drove, places he stopped regularly, when he had lunch, and what time he usually got home. It was extremely handy if the person was single, but generally men had a wife, partner or children, so if he didn't get home at the end of the day roughly when expected, his family would start making calls and, as a last resort, contact the police.

You could never predict what people would do and, even though all our kidnappings were a success, we could never be complacent about even minor details. For instance, someone would always throw a tennis ball at the captive to see which hand he caught it with, so we would know which his dominant hand was.

The vast majority of men we kidnapped were criminals. Some were just on the periphery chancing their arm, but some were seriously heavily involved in importing and dealing vast amounts of hash.

Once we captured our target, we would immediately put a bag over his head and throw him into the boot of a car. It is at that point the reality of what is happening to him hits home.

From the moment he was picked up nobody would speak. Imagine being in complete darkness in the boot of a car, not able to hear a single thing. With every mile the mental torture grows and, after we unloaded him from the car, we would strip him and force him into a new boiler suit. His clothes and footwear were immediately burnt, leaving no evidence of him ever having been at the safe house.

He would then be dragged to the cubby hole under the stairs and given a bottle of water. It wouldn't have achieved anything to hit him, we wanted him to speak, not bleed.

We would rest a cassette player outside the door, playing music loud enough for him not to be able to sleep or think clearly, but also so that he couldn't hear us talking in the house, or know when we approached the door.

The people we took considered themselves big, powerful villains, all bravado and puffed-out chests. However, when you have stripped them of their clothes, they suddenly became pot-bellied, pin-legged mongrels. They completely lose their Tarzan status and the illusion of who they are is gone. You can actually see them lose their body strength. Once they are in a boiler suit, they are completely depersonalised.

No captive ever attempted to scream for help, although we did make it very clear that we would beat the crap out of them if they uttered a word. Occasionally they screamed when they were tortured but, given the nearest neighbour was three-hundred metres away, chances are they wouldn't be heard anyway.

The key was to imply that we actually knew more than we did, or tell a complete lie to understand how much they did know and see if they corrected us. They needed to feel we knew more than we were letting on.

Some of the torture tactics included loading a

pistol next to their head while they had a hood on and then pulling the trigger. We also inflicted waterboarding and kneeling on the back of their neck, but you've really got to know what you're doing as this could cause serious permanent injury or death. Sometimes we argued between ourselves about who was going to do the questioning. That was great fun because we would get really angry with each other. Some of the gang certainly showed signs of being psychopathic. Trust me, the captives were going to answer all our questions after that show.

Once we had gleaned the information and we were satisfied that most of it corresponded with the facts we already knew, we acted. Two of us usually stayed with the kidnapee, while the others went about the task in hand. If it was straightforward and we got a message to say the hash had been picked up, we would immediately release our captive. There is no point in prolonging the agony. We had what we wanted, and some poor sod might actually start missing the great lummox we held captive.

Occasionally, someone might try and be clever, telling us details that weren't strictly accurate, but enough for us to believe. The trouble was we were a cynical bunch, so the moment we were given any new information, we went to find out if it was true.

It doesn't bear thinking about if they had lied. On

a positive note, you knew you would get the truth out of them the second time of asking.

The relief as we silently took them from the cupboard and piled them into the back seat of the car was tangible.

Three of the gang would drop off the captive. One would drive while the other two sat either side of him on the back seat. Despite him being hooded, the gang would don balaclavas as an extra safeguard.

They would drive at least fifty kilometres away from the safe house, making sure they were far enough away from the captive's home to make his return journey long and difficult. He would invariably remain confused and frightened.

All a captive wore was a boiler suit, with nothing on his feet. He would be abandoned on a quiet road with no buildings within sight. Being barefoot meant he couldn't walk quickly, and we knew that, by the time he had found a place to call for help, the gang would be back at the safehouse.

CHAPTER TWENTY-ONE

Most of the gang were at the safehouse when, a couple of hours later, we got a message saying that the rest of the lab contents had been successfully removed.

As soon as we got this news, we dropped the chemists off at their homes. This was highly unusual for us, but they were really amicable and cooperative blokes and also, they were never going to work in Holland again. They had been nicked but had no prison sentence. However, George, with a little help from us, had taken their livelihoods away.

They had no money and no assets and it would take a while for them to get back on their feet in another country, so we really didn't think it was fair to be mean and make them walk.

CHAPTER TWENTY-TWO

The machine the chemists had been using was worth about eighty thousand pounds and could manufacture roughly one pill a second. Given that we already had well over a million available to sell, it was obvious that we couldn't introduce these quantities onto the market all in one go.

Flooding the market would reduce the value, so it was in our interests to drip feed the pills and keep them at a competitive price. However, where do you store nearly thirty sports bags containing roughly two-hundred thousand tablets in each one? By making a friendly approach to ordinary people, actually!

It really was that simple. We asked people we knew if we could rent a cupboard in their home.

Literally.

As long as the cupboard was dry and big enough to hold a sports bag and it was not going to be used, we would pay them fifty thousand guilders a month for their slight inconvenience. Obviously, it had to be agreed that we would lock the cupboard securely and keep the key. We would simply return to take what we needed at a time and day that suited both parties.

There was absolutely no risk for them as we told them that, if ever their houses got raided, which they never were, they had our explicit permission to say that the bags and the contents belonged to our gang.

When you wanted to pick stock up, you had to assume that you were being watched at all times. This may seem slightly paranoid, but it kept you on your toes as you didn't want a nosey neighbour being suspicious of whatever was going on next door.

Having previously double checked the homeowner was in beforehand, I would arrive at the house carrying two strong carrier bags filled with newspapers for the appearance of bulk.

Once inside, and ensuring I wasn't being observed, I would remove the newspapers and fill the same bags with ecstasy, leaving the house with the bags looking exactly as they had when I had entered.

For the equivalent of five hundred pounds a month, the two minutes I was in their house was really good value for money. We didn't keep stock in houses for long, but it did us a huge favour. We now knew people who could be trusted as future contacts to fall back on if necessary.

CHAPTER TWENTY-THREE

The arrangement that we had agreed with Dom was a twenty-five-percent cut, so he was effectively made for life.

Given the enormity of the hash we had taken from his bosses and, let's face it, the shock of it being stolen under the noses of the police, meant there would be some mighty pissed off people around.

As soon as we were free from the warehouse, we asked to meet him.

We had sold some of the hash and decided to give him all that money as he needed it more than we did, but more so, we wanted to meet him so as to give him some good advice.

We were hardened criminals with years of experience between us, not just in the ways of violent robbery and kidnapping, but in human nature. We sat him down and gently advised him what precautions to take. We warned him that, with his first windfall, whatever happened, and we could not emphasise this enough, he should NOT splash the cash.

The last thing he needed to do was draw attention to himself. As he had never done anything like this before, we gently suggested that he lay low, somewhere far away, ideally in another country. He had more than enough money to accomplish this. In fact, his best bet would have been to disappear permanently, and we would send the rest of his share on to him.

There is only so much you can say and advise and, for reasons beyond our logic, he absolutely insisted on staying put and acting as normal. He was convinced that if nothing changed in his mannerisms or method of working, his bosses would not suspect a thing and, when he had all the money from us, he would slip away with his family and never be heard of again.

Obviously, this was his choice, so we clapped him on the back, wished him luck and said we'd be in touch when the next batch of hash was sold.

Chapter Twenty-Four

When any of the gang got a tip, although this usually tended to be Mick and Leon, we would all meet to discuss the proposition. Whoever decided to be in on it got an equal share of the profits. You need to bear in mind that some of the guys had family commitments and other things to sort out, so not everyone got together for these discussions.

On one such occasion, Leon called a meeting and ten of us turned up. He had been approached by a bloke called Fred who happened to be a sea captain, a proper real-life sea captain, with all the right qualifications and years of experience under his belt.

The plan he put to Leon was to buy a sixty-metre freighter, and he already knew of one for sale for 300,000 guilders. Leon, being the optimistic salesman that he was, managed to convince almost everyone what a great investment this would be.

Something just didn't feel quite right but, as everyone else had really bought into the idea, I ignored my instincts and put my hand in too. So we all agreed to hand over 30,000 guilders of our own money.

Before we parted with any cash, it was agreed that we would all meet Fred to hear from the horse's mouth what his grand plan was.

Fred actually seemed like a decent bloke and clearly knew what he was talking about. I even suspect he'd done this kind of thing before, as he spoke like a man of knowledge on the subject of importing hash from various places around the world.

The idea was that he would sail the freighter he was planning to buy with our 300,000 guilders to Pakistan, collect twenty tons of hash and return within two weeks. Fred had already done the deal with the suppliers of the hash but had no means of transport, hence his approach to Leon.

The deal he had struck in Pakistan was for him to take the hash free of charge and, once it had been sold in Holland, he would split his profits fifty-fifty with his new Pakistani friend. That kind of quantity meant we were more than happy for him to have a fifty percent cut, so effectively the ten of us would have a ton of hash each.

All of this sounded good, but I still had a nagging feeling, even when I was handing over my ten percent towards the cost of the freighter.

Fred explained that the route he would be taking

and returning by, would allow us to see the ship from the east coast of our patch, near the Hook of Holland in a place called Dead Hook, because you couldn't get any radio signal in that small area. He gave us a realistic time line of fourteen to sixteen days before he would be back. The freighter had a tracking number, so we could plot where it would be at any given time.

The plan was, once he was sailing back and in our sights from land, we would connect with him at an agreed place at sea. We would ride to meet him on Zodiacs which are inflatable and very stable speed boats. We would unload the hash within the Dead Hook area, speed to shore and then transfer it into various cars on land, which in turn would take it away to store safely.

It wouldn't take more than an hour to unload into the Zodiacs and then the freighter would sail on to Rotterdam.

There is no point in worrying until you've got something to worry about. The group knew I wasn't happy with the deal and tried to reassure me. I knew the whole thing was out of our hands until the ship came back into view roughly a fortnight later.

On day twelve, I decided to hide in some dunes with a perfect view of the Hook with a pair of binoculars and watch and wait. And wait.

I lay there for hours and hours each day,

monitoring the place where the freighter was meant to pass. I did this every day for a further week, feeling increasingly unsettled, especially as we had tracking of the ship in our vicinity, but no sighting of it. As far as anyone could tell, it looked like Fred had sailed away from our horizon and docked at another port and there was nothing we could do but sit it out and wait to hear from him.

It was just over three weeks later before he made contact with Leon, who told him to meet at his house later that evening.

By now all of the gang involved were extremely pissed off. I was the last to arrive and decided to vent my anger and frustration by punching Fred, which resulted in him being knocked to the floor although, sadly, not knocked out. No one stopped me because I had just done what they all wanted to do. We needed to hear his side of the story and then, effectively, kidnap him if needs be.

Fred picked himself off the floor, for the first time actually looking like he knew he was in trouble. To our amazement, he had made contact because he needed our help.

The guy was either a complete fool or had real balls to turn up and face us.

It transpired that Fred had not been paid by The Adder, who was the boss who had ordered the hash from Pakistan in the first place. Fred had trusted him, but Adder saw him as a fool who had gone to the trouble to buy a ship, so Adder himself had no outlay and little risk until the container was past customs and unloaded. In effect Fred had been hijacked and now had no money to repay us, or any hash to trade.

This story sounded far-fetched and well-rehearsed, as if he'd spent the last three weeks going over it time and again.

It didn't matter how much detail he gave us, something just wasn't sitting right. With no deliberation necessary, we decided to take the matter into our own hands. We told him he was going to stay with us until we could check out his story.

After a couple of days asking around, we discovered a very different version of events.

It would appear that Fred had already orchestrated a deal with another gang in Amsterdam, led by The Adder who wouldn't fork out for the ship, so he had suggested Fred found the money himself and then he could get a cut of the hash once he had got it through customs.

Being short of the money, Fred had sought out Leon knowing that, if he could sell the idea to him, there would be a reasonable chance that a few more of our gang would chip in.

We were thinking of chipping Fred into tiny

pieces. He'd had no intention of delivering the hash to us once he had the transport organised.

Not only had he double-crossed us, but worse, he had treated us like fools. Now was the time to get proper answers and information about how we could reach Adder to have a word.

Adder, quite understandably, was a tricky man to find. He was well known in Amsterdam and was a suspected murderer. Put it this way, the police knew he was responsible for the disappearance of several people, but they had nothing on him, so he was free to carry on being a ball-ache.

Luckily Adder's right-hand man was more accessible and, having got a name, description and rough idea as to where to find him, we put a call in to Tipp and a few of us made our way to Rotterdam where we headed for a bistro, thought to be his regular haunt.

We weren't asking for the moon on a stick. All we wanted was our money back, nothing more, nothing less. We had resigned ourselves to the fact that the hash had gone to a rival in Amsterdam, but we had a point to make and we weren't going to be a pushover for the investment we had made.

It wasn't until much later on in the proceedings that it was apparent that The Adder had never heard of us and, when one of his henchmen did mention us, he flapped his hand as if swatting away a fly. We were clearly of no importance or relevance and, as far as he was concerned, being a member of a gang that didn't have a leader made us look rather weak. He probably thought we should learn from our mistakes and, if that meant kissing goodbye to 300,000 guilders, then so be it.

To say he underestimated us, is something of an understatement.

Adder's right-hand man was called Jay Park and, luckily for us, he was a creature of habit. Tipp knew the patch well, so we spent a few days getting to know the streets and one-way systems, and the locations of all the usual places to avoid. That knowledge cut our surveillance time in half, so a couple of days later we made our move.

As we expected, the right-hand man was enjoying an espresso in a bistro. However, on this occasion, he had decided to meet a friend and bring along his pet dog, a lovely Border collie.

Some of the gang stayed outside in their own cars, ready to block all roads if needs be. Four of us, dressed as the IRA, stormed into the bistro. Nobody moved. We were in complete control of the situation from the second we got inside. The men knew we were there for them, and sensibly did not resist.

We were back outside with both men and the dog within fifteen seconds. They were immediately separated and put into different cars. No one called the police.

One of the reasons we sometimes dressed as IRA was the combination of fear and awe of their status in Holland and Belgium at that time. An incident in 1990 had seen three people, believed to be members of the IRA, flee from police to seek refuge in a forest. Two were quickly caught but the remaining man lasted for a further week on his wits and survival instincts. This gave him a new-found respect in the Netherlands and made the Dutch extremely wary of this organisation.

We knew word would get back to Adder, so we wanted him to believe he was dealing with the IRA.

The second man was of no use to us so, when we were away from prying eyes, we removed his shoes and let him go. He would not be able to identify us and there was little point in keeping someone who was no threat to Adder and no use to us.

We drove Jay and his dog to the safe house, took all his identity documents, stripped him and put him in a boiler suit. As it happened, Jay was calm and cooperative, but clearly not used to being kidnapped. As he had put up no resistance, there seemed little point in tying him up. The cubby hole was just big enough for a person to stand up in, so he could move around a little.

It was decided that only one of us should speak, feed and water Jay. Given I had the most impressive

Irish accent I got the job.

One of my particular favourite bands at the time was Vaya Con Dios, so I played their greatest hits all day and all night just outside the cubby hole to maximise sleep deprivation. I turned the volume down at night as I didn't want anyone being drawn to the noise. He only ever saw me in overalls and a balaclava and heard me speaking in an Irish accent, so he had no reason to believe I wasn't part of the IRA.

The following day, Leon took the dog to the Rotterdam Football Club. In the car park was a row of poplars, so he tethered the dog to one of them. He managed to get a message to Jay's wife, once he was clear of the club, to tell her where his dog was. We were actually quite sad to see the dog go as it really was a lovely Border collie.

Sadly for our victim, it took Fred three weeks to come up with the goods. He had been communicating with Adder through a couple of his thugs and, because we didn't go away and were determined to keep Jay for as long as it took to get our money back, we agreed to be paid in hash.

The pre-planned meeting place was at a lovely old pub called The Golden Lion. To maintain our front, we were dressed identically in overalls, wearing the same boots and carrying the same guns. We outnumbered them by four to one. Jamal had a habit of dropping his gun, which didn't do our street credibility much good, and we were more than surprised when he managed to hold the damn thing for the duration of the handover.

They had brought two hundred-and-forty kilos of hash which was sitting in the back of an unmarked van. Unfortunately, it had also been sitting in water, so the hash had a white fungus growing over it, making it effectively worthless. We did show willing as one of our team attempted to scrape the mould off with a wire brush. However, given we had endured so much hassle from these clowns, we decided to refuse to take it as payment. Knowing that they really couldn't be trusted, we demanded to be repaid in cash.

As we knew a lot of people, we later discovered that the ruined hash had been sent to England and sold there. Says a lot about the Brits really, I suppose.

We met again a few days later at the same venue, where they paid us in pounds sterling. We double-checked that the notes weren't forged and did a rough calculation to work out that the exchange rate would just about repay us with a small profit. But a deal is a deal, so we accepted the money. As I was the only Brit in the team, it was down to me to take the cash to the bank. It took bloody ages to exchange as I couldn't afford to raise suspicion, so I had to get it converted to guilders over several weeks across most of Holland.

When we freed Jay, he had no idea where he was. He was released at night, barefoot and blindfolded.

What I failed to mention were the things the gang got up to while I was baby-sitting Jay. Obviously, I was kept fully up to date, but my specific job was to ensure our kidnapped man was safe and well, albeit shit scared and desperate to get home.

One thing you have to know is who you're dealing with. It gets you nowhere if you are in the dark about the character you are trying to negotiate with. For this reason, four of the gang went to Jay's house and had a damn good look around.

Obviously, they had all his personal details, including a front door key. They watched the house for a while and logged the daily habits of his wife. They let themselves in when they knew they would have at least two hours without being interrupted. They actually worked so efficiently that they were in and out within a quarter of an hour, leaving them wiggle room to deal with anything unexpected.

It just so happened that The Adder had recently got married. Not only did he have a new wife, but he had invited everyone in the top echelons of his mob to the wedding. Even better, he had gone to the trouble of having the event videoed, with sound, and had taken a whole stack of photographs too.

Jay also had details of all the business contacts they had dealt with over the past decade and, by all accounts, records of all the trade and profits.

Knowing that much of the stuff around his house had been bought from proceeds of crime made it easy pickings for the gang and, frankly, if you are going to be kidnapped for a month, you'll hand anything over to make your life easier in captivity.

We would allow Jay to speak to his wife, so she realised he was okay. Well, as okay as anyone can be under the circumstances, but also that she felt there really was a likelihood that he would be released relatively unharmed. That was our plan from the start. I mean, we're not all bad.

The gang went through everything they had collected from Jay's house. From the wedding video we knew the names everyone was called, both their real names and any nicknames. We knew what they looked and sounded like. We knew who their partners were, what they preferred to drink, how many children they had, and of course we knew all about The Adder.

Now that is going to hurt. Suddenly, we were the ones with the power, and he was vulnerable, but at this stage he didn't know it. He had paid us what we asked for because he knew he had to and, although he hadn't been double-crossed by Jay, it had slowly but deliciously, for us, dawned on him that he was one man dependent on others, while we were a solid team who could depend totally on each other.

It is so nice when things work out that way.

So, a month after we had let Jay free, we now knew all there was to know about Adder's motley crew. We had asked for nothing more than the money we were down at the start of this farce, but boy did we now have the drop on Adder. He was belly up and balls exposed, and he didn't know what to make of us.

He also still truly believed we were the IRA.

Chapter Twenty-Five

It must have been a month since we had released Jay, and he was back in the fold of Adder's team.

Back in the day, people used to have their weekly or monthly subscription magazines delivered to their door. Holland wasn't big on letter boxes, so post was left in boxes on the outside of the building or at the end of the drive. However, periodicals were a bit too bulky, so these were left in bright orange or yellow carrier bags and hung on the door handle.

This may sound daft in today's world, but no one ever touched them. It was just the accepted norm.

Jay loved a bit of rest and relaxation with clock making, or trainspotting, and had a monthly drop.

His wife was out on this particular Saturday when her husband's magazines were delivered and popped onto the door handle. He returned home with some shopping and removed the bag from the handle. On impact he was blown into a thousand pieces and splattered over a fifty-metre radius.

That's what becomes of you if you are stupid

enough to get caught by a gang who can steal enough evidence to get your boss locked away for a hundred years.

The Adder still has never been convicted of Jay's murder, even though the police know he was behind the bombing.

CHAPTER TWENTY-SIX

We'd had no need to contact Dom but, about a week after we'd advised him to disappear, he called Leon and asked if he could meet him. There was no point in being mob-handed as Leon wasn't in any danger, so he informed us when and where he was meeting Dom and we simply left them to it.

Dom was asking for more money. He had been a little heavy-handed with his spending, but his bosses hadn't suspected a thing, so he knew he had made the right decision in staying put and continuing to work. All he needed was a few thousand guilders as he was planning his move away at the end of the month. In fact his wife, although initially very concerned about Dom's safety, was now looking forward to a change of scenery.

Leon explained that they hadn't sold any more of the hash but, as a favour he said he would help him out and give him what he asked for from his own pocket.

He also gently explained that Dom should not be

complacent, and perhaps he should think about moving his plans to the end of the day, rather than the week or month. They chatted for about half an hour and Dom left delighted that Leon had helped out. He said he would think about his advice.

Leon asked Dom to be discreet when he next contacted him with his new address and once again wished him luck.

Chapter Twenty-Seven

A few days after this chat with Dom, Leon was approached in a coffee bar by a thoroughly pissed-off employee of a local money lender. Well, more of a money launderer really, which is just the type of customer we liked to fleece.

The mark, Lucas, lived in a stunning three-storey town house at the wealthy end of town so we knew it would be an easy steal. However, we weren't complacent and went to do a recce to see what we were up against.

There was no point waiting once we understood everything about Lucas and his business activities. We decided we would drop by at the end of the week on a Friday evening.

This good-mannered, respectable man with his high-profile and well-bred friends and clients, was adept at moving money around until it was completely clean. This meant he had money at his fingertips throughout his house in various international currencies.

The employee of Lucas was more pissed off than we realised, and we agreed a twenty-five percent cut for all the information we needed. Lucas fronted his dealings by working in various financial fields such as insurance or trading on the Stock Exchange. Basically, he worked at anything where he could deal in money. We knew he would have been very wary of the police or any authority that could see through how he had obtained his dubious wealth.

So, the day we decided to make a visit we were clean-shaven in smart police uniforms and all armed with identical guns.

Entry was quick. I stood by the front door while two others ushered the family into one large downstairs lounge. They had two young boys, aged around six or seven, who were free to run around and clearly enjoying the sudden change of plan for the evening.

Two of the gang stationed on the street couldn't and didn't stop normal activity, despite the fact more and more people were coming to the house. Some had flowers or wine and it was clear we had picked the one evening our target was throwing a party.

One of his sons was intensely curious and approached me to ask what we were doing there. Then he wanted to see my ID badge to check if I looked anything like my picture. Sadly, I knew I couldn't lay a finger on any child, even the most godawful precocious one. The kid knew my reaction wasn't that of a real police officer and ran off to tell his mother this.

Despite not having any official ID or search warrants, the adults had no reason to believe we weren't the police, so it didn't matter what the parents thought. All their friends attending the party were herded into the same room, where drinks continued to be poured and air-kisses exchanged.

We knew our time was limited because of this exposure and they all had mobile phones, so the rest of the gang flew through the house looking in all the obvious places where money and possessions would be stored. We were out and away within fifteen minutes with about 7,500,000 in guilders (about £75,000). Our target knew he couldn't make a fuss because, as far as he was concerned, the police were taking laundered money.

To this day we don't know if he cottoned on that we were baddies taking his goodies, but as long as he wasn't arrested and dobbed in by his kids, he wouldn't really care.

CHAPTER TWENTY-EIGHT

The police knew who each of the gang members were and what we looked like. I was the one and only Pommie, so they would sometimes hang around in bars known to be frequented by mainly English people. They would fit in and look and behave like part of the crowd, trying to glean any information, no matter how trivial, in the hopes of building a case against me. Credit where it's due, they made an effort, even though it was a pointless effort because they had nothing else to go on, and never did in the entire time I was in their country.

The key thing is to be grey. You need to ensure you never draw attention to yourself. You need to blend in, look ordinary and wear clothes like the locals do. It's the same with any cars you drive. Never be a smart ass or make your presence felt by screeching brakes or gear crunching. Admittedly, you might be driving a tad on the quick side, but it should be safe, quick driving.

The other great advantage with driving in

Holland was left-wheel drive. It is surprisingly much easier to steer quickly, and you can have a walkie-talkie or gun in one hand and drive with the other.

Anyway, it just so happened that Mick had a cousin who was nicknamed The Manager. He was a big fat, sweaty gypsy, about thirty-five years old and, although morbidly obese, he was pretty agile and active.

He wore his hard-earned cash on his wrist and neck and brandished gold Rolex watches to prove to others what a big powerful, wealthy man he was. The volume and size of the gold necklaces he wore made him look like a Mr. T starter kit. He operated as a go-between, so brought weed into Holland, sometimes to export, but more often than not to sell in both in his local area and much further afield into other gang territories.

We robbed him of his weed five times over the years. He never knew it was us, even though he was Mick's neighbour. He would occasionally complain to him, confused as to how anyone could possibly know where to find his stash of hash, especially as he rarely stored it in the same place twice.

The Manager generally sold quantities of about two to three-hundred kilos at a time. He was not a street dealer, which made it really worthwhile robbing him. The key was to find out where the transactions took place. However, like many fairly switched-on felons, he made it somewhere bleeding obvious by choosing locations where he would not stand out or look conspicuous. The local large supermarket car park was an ideal place.

The money side of things would be exchanged a little distance away in a quiet area unseen by anyone. Then The Manager would turn up towards the rear of the car park and hand over the hash in shopping bags. These would be transferred to the boot of an average household car. The buyers would look like blokes who were shopping. There was no bling, no smoked car windows, flash tyres, bright cars or anything that would draw attention to them.

The proper shoppers would be too busy doing their own thing and, if they chose to look up, they would simply see a couple of blokes putting shopping from one car to another. Two minutes later the car would have driven sedately from the supermarket. Nothing to see here, thank you very much.

There would be a couple of us watching this unfold. Our contact was one of the middle men who worked with The Manager. So, every time a deal was on the cards, he would let us know where and when. It was always at very short notice, so we would be paged and then scramble to the handover point.

On one occasion we followed the van a short distance on its way to the supermarket and, as The Manager paused at a junction, we made our move. Sadly, it wasn't ideal. It happened to be across the road from a school. We were all dressed identically, in dark blue boiler suits, police boots and balaclavas, and carrying full-size Uzis with silencers across our bodies.

A teacher and children, who had witnessed us stopping the van, actually remained outside to see what the commotion was all about. I happened to be facing the school so, while the others got on with the job in hand, I held up my driving licence and shouted that we were the police and advised her to go back inside the building. You couldn't tell from that distance if it was a warrant card, credit card or library card. She simply believed what she was seeing and conformed immediately.

Most of the time The Manager would have done his deal and handed over the hash before we could reach the destination, but it made sense to follow him in his empty van, in case he drove back to the place where he had stored his batch of hash. This didn't work every time but occasionally, when it did, we literally took it from there.

Over a few years we must have taken thousands of kilos of hash from him, and each time Mick would quietly sit listening to his misfortune, as he was still unable to fathom how he had been caught by a gang he knew nothing about. He knew Mick was part of a gang, but it never occurred to him he might have been involved.

At the end of the day, our success enabled us to keep one step ahead of everyone and it continued mainly because of our meticulous preparation. We always ensured we had five or six plans, so if anything happened that we weren't expecting, or circumstances suddenly changed, we could communicate through walkie-talkies and move to another plan in an instant, still able to carry out the robbery or kidnap or, as a rare last resort, abort the plan and get out without being caught.

You have to bear in mind the police only had one plan, so if they were fed duff information, or followed the wrong gang member, or turned up at the wrong place, they had nothing to fall back on. It's easy when you know how.

CHAPTER TWENTY-NINE

Some deals may take a great deal of time to plan and then nothing comes of them for a variety of reasons, sometimes because of the death of a pivotal contact. That tends to put a tin hat on everything, but actually most deals did work out because of our scrupulous groundwork and the element of violence and surprise.

When a deal had paid dividends, we really enjoyed spending the money.

Quite often this involved eating out. Sometimes our raucous behaviour would drive other diners from the restaurant. Owners would dread our arrival because it affected their business for weeks afterwards. However, we were big tippers and, in the unlikely event anything got damaged or broken, we more than compensated for it in cash.

We also indulged in holidays and spoiling our loved ones. Very occasionally things would go quiet on the hash and ecstasy front, so we would run a little low on funds. My idea of 'a little low on funds' was being down to my last twenty thousand pounds.

We always made a profit on our rip deals. Even the disaster involving The Adder gave us a little profit. We could spend a month kidnapping people to get the information we needed to do a rip deal and, at the last minute, something could change like a switch of venue, country, dock, or warehouse. Occasionally the police might get wind of something going down and set up surveillance, in which case all we could do was back away. You have to take the rough with the smooth.

We weren't getting any attention from the police either. They knew about us, who we were and where we lived, but they had nothing on us. It probably helped that we were building a reputation for not killing anyone, and only stealing from other criminals. We had minimal contact with, and posed no threat to the general public. Obviously, they weren't happy, but while they were trying to build their case against us, they would leave us well alone.

Local Bobbies were even told not to give us a parking ticket or be too fussed if they caught one of us speeding the wrong way down a one-way street in reverse. Obviously, we didn't know this at the time, but the longer we ruled the streets, the more blind eyes we were getting from the police.

As the years passed, the general public were becoming aware of us and, if any of them found themselves in a café when a fracas broke out, or somebody was being encouraged to leave to be kidnapped, they all stayed put and no one called the police. Mind you, it was rare that these interruptions lasted more than about five minutes.

Put it this way, if anyone did call the police, there was more than a reasonable chance that we would have made off before they arrived. Also, it was more than likely that they would know we were dealing with some other gang trying to muscle in, or some low life who owed us money. So they would put it down to a misunderstanding and not bother to arrest us.

One week when we were all feeling a bit light on funds, by a happy coincidence, Mick received a tip that something was going down in the east of Holland, close to the German border. This was not our territory, but needs must, so we popped along with no notice or planning to see what was going on.

We turned up in two cars at a quiet car park and caught men in the act of transferring goods and cash from one vehicle to another. Unfortunately it was already dark and raining heavily, so we couldn't make out who was the buyer and who was the seller. We were in totally unfamiliar surroundings and then, to our complete surprise, a third car pulled up.

Suddenly one man left his car, stepped into another and drove off at the exact same time that one of the two cars we had been watching also sped off.

The two cars exited the car park in different directions, so we had no idea which car had the hash. This separation put us at a disadvantage as we didn't know where we were, or who we were dealing with. I made a snap decision and turned left.

Luckily the others followed, so we remained close enough to communicate. However, it became apparent that we had to stop the car we were pursuing really quickly.

In these situations, we had to assume that the men we were following had mobiles so, if they suspected anything, they could easily call others to come and help. We succeeded in stopping them within a mile of leaving the car park simply by switching a blue light on. The ball ache was the light had to be operated manually.

Glory be and thanks to all mankind, the car pulled over immediately. This made us think that we'd picked the wrong car. I stayed put while keeping the blue light flashing, while the other car pulled in front to prevent the two men inside getting away. They had no reason to believe we were not the police.

There was nothing in the car we had chased. Both men were unarmed and one of them had ID showing his address. We decided to escort him to his flat, because there was a reasonable chance there would be something there of use to us. I mean, we'd got this far, so we might as well see it through.

While Boon and I took our man back to his home, the rest of our group put his colleague in the boot of their car, parked out of the way of prying eyes. There is nothing more suspicious than four men in a car, after dark, parked in a well-lit street full of houses.

The apartment block our man lived in was about six storeys tall and his flat was on the fourth floor. Two of us accompanied him. I was the one gripping the hair at the back of his head with one hand, while pressing a Glock to the nape of his neck with the other. His hands were dangling free in front of him.

When I asked him how many people were inside his flat, he told me two. The moment he admitted this I knew he was lying and that the flat would be empty. Human nature is that people wouldn't put others at risk, especially when they would have been outnumbered and unlikely to be armed.

The other two of our group had got ahead of us and were waiting to enter the flat. I insisted the prisoner lead the way, so he acted as a human shield. I could have shot around him in the unlikely event that someone was in the flat waiting for us. When I opened the door, we were standing in a small corridor which led to the kitchen. On a low coffee table lay an open newspaper. The next thing I heard was the paper being moved, while our prisoner simultaneously shouted:

'I've got a grenade, the pin is out, boys.'

In a split second, I threw my gun behind me, put my arms around his waist and grabbed his hands, covering them completely in mine, so he couldn't throw the grenade. I shouted for someone to knock him out and immediately Boon pistol-whipped him, so he fell limp in my arms. I carefully retrieved the grenade and put the pin back into it. The grenade was about the size of a lemon, and because the lever hadn't been triggered the grenade remained safe as I reinserted the pin.

For years this was the closest I had been to death. In the movies people can run or throw clear a grenade, but this is not how they work. We would have been blown to smithereens. The fact our captive didn't care about dying himself showed the character we were dealing with.

Boon was an enormous lump of a man with incredible strength, and he was beyond fury. Our man started making noises as he came round and, with his rage almost palpable, Boon picked him up and ran at the glass-fronted oven, using his head as a battering ram. The force was so great his head smashed the oven door into a thousand pieces.

Now that was going to hurt.

While we thought he might not come round for a couple of minutes, the four of us searched his apartment. One thing we never did was fling things around. I mean we didn't need it to look like a burglary and, if you are neat, you are less likely to miss something important, so we were incredibly fast but efficient.

We looked in the most obvious places. These were usually bedside cabinet drawers that we checked underneath as well, also the back and top of the wardrobe and any suitcases. In the early 1990s most people had a landline phone and would often keep their contacts or Filofax next to it. Under the pillows was usually the place for weapons. We also removed the kitchen unit kickboards and then looked in the toilet cistern and the freezer for cash.

We were done in two minutes flat, just in time to hear our man coming round. Three of us dragged him from the flat, while the fourth established where the others were with the other man.

We met up in under a minute and drove for a further five until we came to a quiet, off-the-beaten-track area, with a small copse of trees. The nearest village was about five kilometres away. It was now one in the morning.

The wanker who had removed the pin from the grenade was now safely in my care and, despite Boon's best efforts to try and slow him down, I decided I was now going to ensure this happened. Nothing was going to give me greater pleasure than to shoot him in the knee, at an angle to cause maximum pain with a real possibility he would lose part of his leg.

He was already positioned in a kneeling stance and my gun was cocked. I was within a nanosecond of pulling the trigger when two women suddenly appeared on 'sit up and beg' bikes, peddling on the nearby cycle path. As they rode, we caught them saying, deliberately for us to hear, 'we haven't seen anything, we haven't seen anything, we haven't seen anything', as they continued cycling as fast as they could.

They saved this man his knee and, almost certainly, his life. Between us we were all thinking, 'What hadn't they seen?' Taking this as a cue to leave, we dumped the men, taking their shoes from them and abandoning them to their fate.

We had managed to secure some money, hash and the hand grenade. It was certainly enough to have made the trip worthwhile. Now that my temper had died down, I was relieved that I hadn't fired my gun. We were out of our patch and unknown to gangs in this area so, although we'd left a bloody mess behind, no one had died and the only thing that needed replacing was a glass oven door.

Chapter Thirty

All of the gang had partners. Some were married, some had girlfriends and, naturally, some had both. We tended to work during the winter months and enjoy our spoils during the summer. We kept in touch if we needed to, but mostly we kept ourselves to ourselves and got on with enjoying a summer break and catching up with other friends and family.

It was just coming into spring in Holland, which is a beautiful time of year, when a punter called Henning made an approach to Leon. He had been owed money for some considerable time by an Englishman who had an apartment in a rather nice area of Spain called Puerto Banús. This is a luxury marina and shopping complex located in the area of Nueva Andalucía to the southwest of Marbella, on the Costa del Sol.

After a deal was struck with Leon to retrieve what we could in cash and assets, a few of us set about recovering his debt for him. Any excuse to visit Puerto Banús for a few days wasn't all bad.

No matter where I was in the world, I would always leave it to the last minute to buy a plane ticket. I was known to the police and, as they like nothing better than having an excuse to stop me, booking in advance would have given them a reason to show up at the airport. There was also little point in using a false passport while I was doing nothing wrong or carrying anything suspicious.

With the plane to Spain scheduled to leave at eleven in the morning and, with only a small amount of hand luggage on me, I entered Rotterdam airport at nine-thirty, bought a ticket with cash, and boarded the flight. Paying with cash is always going to flag you up, but it is less of a risk from a small airport like Rotterdam or City of London, which were the places I tended to use the most.

The other three joined the trip using different modes of transport and at different times of the day. We had arranged to meet early evening at a block of apartments overlooking the marina. We wanted to see if any were available to rent for a week. Again, we didn't pre-book for obvious reasons.

Luck was on our side. We all looked the part, wearing high-end bespoke clothing with pastel-coloured jumpers casually slung over our shoulders. Looking at us, you would think we each owned a yacht. The manager was suitably impressed, especially when we asked for a large waterfront flat, for which we would pay handsomely in cash, as long as he didn't feel the need to register our names and arrival.

The money went straight into his pocket, and we went straight to the penthouse.

Every piece of personal information that might identify us was locked in the safe. All we had on us was cash, with no fancy watches or jewellery, just smart clothes that made us blend in with the in-crowd.

The conman we were after was an Englishman called Ralph. We had recent pictures of him, so knew who we were looking for. He owned a company based in Puerto Banús that sold jet skis and other water sports paraphernalia. By all accounts he worked from an office at home which was in a substantial property with a waterfront view.

Leon had been in touch with Ralph by phone to discuss a deal which was big enough to get his attention. They agreed to meet at Malaga airport a week later, with a view to spending a few days in each other's company, trying out the stock and thrashing out a deal. This also gave us time to find out as much as possible about our man.

The other two, making up the four, were Hans and Buck.

Hans was very good-looking with blonde hair. The trouble was, he knew it and played up to it.

Because of his looks he had slipped on his education, so he was amazingly stupid and had very little common sense. Although he was an asset and a bit of a distraction where women were concerned, there wasn't much going for him. Actually that's not really fair, he did have incredibly good co-ordination and was excellent on a motorbike so, whenever we needed a decoy or an incredibly quick getaway, Hans was our man.

Leon had given Ralph a cover story explaining that he was part of a gang and he intended to smuggle jet skis into Morocco. He went into significant detail about how we would manage this, while subtly understating how much money would be in it for him. Leon explained the risks involved for both parties but further detailed what we planned to do to minimise these. We needed to appeal to his sense of greed, but also wanted to spend sufficient time with him to put him completely at ease.

Ralph had told Leon he was flying in from Belgium, thinking this would make Leon think he lived there. He needn't have bothered as we already knew his home address in England, what his house looked like, and we had all the details of his wife and children. However, we let him think we believed he lived in Belgium. He had a car at the airport car park, which we understood was one of the items that needed to be recovered. Ralph still hadn't attempted to pay Henning, instead he just made promises of money he was intending to pay at some point in the future.

The four of us arrived and entered Malaga airport from separate places, watching keenly for Ralph who appeared within ten minutes with a friend. We swooped immediately, nudging his companion out of the way and overwhelming Ralph, with all of us talking at once. Leon introduced himself, Hans took his hand luggage from him, while I took his car keys, saying he must be tired after his flight, and I would be more than happy to chauffeur him.

To my delight, the car was a new bright red Mercedes 350 diesel, so we all got in, with Ralph squashed between Buck and Hans in the back seat.

The one thing you can say about the four of us is that we were good company. True to our word, we discussed our potential for buying jet skis and went into great detail about the Moroccan market. Every day we would turn up at Ralph's house and spend hours trying different skis and enjoying long leisurely lunches. By the third day he was completely relaxed and felt like one of the lads.

It was on the fourth day that Leon turned up on his own and gently and quietly enlightened Ralph as to the real reason for our visit. His voice was calm and tempered while he explained that we were simply going to take everything he owned and, as long as he agreed, we would not harm a hair on his head or do anything to his wife and children in England. On top of this, once we had walked away with all his worldly goods we would not look back and he would never hear from any of us ever again.

Oddly enough, he agreed immediately. At this point the rest of us entered the house and sifted through each room thoroughly, getting all the supporting paperwork for the jet skis, car and watches, as we had already given the heads-up to Pig who was finding buyers in Holland for our booty.

Leon drove the Mercedes back while we arranged transport for the rest of the gear. We didn't make a great deal of money, but we had a lot of fun and we never heard from, or about, Ralph again.

Chapter Thirty-One

It was always nice to receive good tips, and we were especially pleased when Leon called us to a meeting to see if we wanted to remove twenty-five million guilders' worth of hash from a delightful drug dealer called Lars, based in Rotterdam. This represented about a quarter of a million pounds.

According to our grass, his stash was stored in his garage at home. He lived on the smarter side of town. His house was on a very expensive and trendy estate, surrounded by similar middle class neighbours. His business front was banking, which certainly had a ring of truth about it because, once he sold his hash, he would have had to put the money somewhere. Some was probably under his bed, but most we were sure would make it, when it was sparkly clean, into a bank account, doubtless in his wife's name.

The first thing we did was reconnoitre the area from his house, encompassing a five-mile radius so we could establish the exit routes each of us would take. We also picked out a suitable meeting place for the end of the theft, as it was more than likely we would need to separate, especially if the police chased us.

The plan was that Hans would drive the car with the hash, and I was going to be his wingman, directing him.

Completely satisfied with the plan, we decided to pay Lars a visit on what was a glorious sunny Sunday early afternoon. Birds were singing, people were setting up barbecues, children were playing, and neighbours were mowing their lawns. It was a perfect weekend scene.

Chris, being six foot five and lean as a pole, was clearly the man to deal with Lars. As it happened our con was about the same proportions. I didn't see how Chris had picked him up, as I was busy packing the car with hash from the garage, but it would have been a surprising and remarkably quick attack. We were pleased that our grass was accurate about the amount of hash to expect to find, and it seemed as if the plan was coming together.

Now Chris's favourite way of holding people was by putting his thumb in the victim's ear while holding the back of his head with the rest of his hand. We are talking big hands and palms here. He hadn't handcuffed the con, because of his secure grip and, understandably, no one had ever been able to get free from Chris's grip. Until now.

The car we were using was a Nissan 4.2 six-cylinder manual jeep and, as Hans was doing the driving, he wasn't armed, although I had a SIG Sauer and a Philips screwdriver.

Just as we were loading the last couple of hash blocks into the jeep, the serene idyll was shattered. Lars had somehow managed to escape Chris's grip and was simultaneously screaming, wailing and running up the street, flailing his arms and shouting to all and sundry that he was being kidnapped and was running for his life.

You could see neighbours dropping what they were doing and going inside to call the police. We couldn't hang around and we were just grateful that Chris had held him long enough for us to take and pack all the hash. We splintered off in five different directions.

Boon was a great lump of a bloke, and he looked quite incongruous on a bike, but he was a hell of a decoy. He had been brought into the gang by Tipp, but he proved to be a liar. After he had served time for being caught with coke, we decided to tolerate him. However, when he got caught a second time he became a risk too far, so he had to leave us immediately.

Anyway, it didn't take a genius to realise that probably one of the worst getaway cars is a Nissan

Patrol 4.2 turbo manual short-wheel-base jeep. It couldn't scrape the skin off a rice pudding, and it didn't help having the two hundred and forty kilos of hash in the back.

In Holland, when police received this type of emergency call, they would immediately drive to well-positioned places to intercept or block off roads entirely. They knew that to leave the region you would have to pass at least one of them. They also drove Porsche Carrera 911s, so they had a reasonable chance of catching whoever they were after.

Lars' house was close to a dual carriageway so, within five minutes, we were behind one another and blending in with the speeds of the cars surrounding us. You don't want to stand out by speeding, especially as Lars' neighbours, who had called the police, couldn't identify any of the cars that had left the scene except for the jeep, which unfortunately for us, was where all the hash was.

So, we were all together and, as luck would have it, Boon on his motor bike had pulled in directly behind Hans and me and he was also sticking to the speed of the surrounding traffic, so as not to be conspicuous. Suddenly, an unmarked Honda Civic, driven by plain clothes policemen shot past us like a bat out of hell, clearly expecting that we would be putting our foot to the floor. There is something quite satisfying in watching a frantic chase unfold when you are just minding your own business doing ninety kilometres an hour in the middle lane.

However, they must have twigged not long after, as they pulled over and waited for the traffic to pass by which, sadly, included us. We were spotted immediately and, as the police Honda pulled out, we knew the chase was on.

We headed for Dead Hook, because there was no radio signal there, so we could stop the police detailing exactly where they were. It didn't matter that we couldn't talk to the gang, it just mattered that we got clear with the gear.

To reach Dead Hook we had to go through an underpass about a quarter of a mile long. It was a tricky narrow road with no overtaking and, just as we entered the tunnel, Boon pootled out a hundred meters in front of the speeding Honda, obeying the speed limit of 60kph on his bike. No amount of bad language and threats from the police was going to move Boon. He was observing the highway-code and that was that. This gave us the head start we needed, even though it wasn't for long.

Unbeknown to us, one of the main roads we had planned to travel on had had temporary roadworks set up only that morning, so we doubled back on ourselves and passed the police as they raced towards us. Hand gestures were exchanged as we pelted over a fifty-foot grass embankment which led straight onto a works' road. The only way to stop was to career into a banner at the bottom.

We rarely got followed in these circumstances and we honestly thought that would be the end of the chase. However, these coppers were determined. They had us in their sights and nothing was going to stop them.

Well, nothing except a Nissan jeep reversing over twenty meters at breakneck speed into the front of a Honda Civic. We smashed their police car to pieces and drove off to our pre-planned destination. I could see in the wing mirror a smouldering engine and an equally smouldering copper, who, if I wasn't mistaken, was gesturing something very unfavourable in our direction.

The meeting place was close to a small private block of houses that had parking spots at the back of them. Hans reversed the car into a parking space so the damage to the boot couldn't be seen. The estate was near some woods, so we buried our guns in holes in the trees, leaving the covered hash in the car. Then we walked a mile to a café, in a beautiful spot, and waited to be collected.

One thing that will make you look guilty of a crime involving stolen hash is having the hash and any weapons together, so it is always important to separate the two.

A couple of the team found the jeep and transported the hash back to one of their homes. A few hours after we had reached the café, Boon picked us up in his BMW and we returned to the woods and retrieved our guns. Then we made our way home. The police were searching for the cars and the bike involved in the robbery, but they were safely tucked away. Boon actually passed some police cruising around but, despite wanting to, I decided not to wave to them. Mind you, I have to say, that was the closest the police had ever got to catching us in a chase.

Chapter Thirty-Two

Obviously, we were well known as a gang but, apart from Leon, who insisted on being seen as the big team leader, we weren't recognised when we went out.

A gang based in Manchester, England, had a contact on our patch who organised their ecstasy supplies and it seemed he was now becoming a problem. The Mancunians had recently paid their middleman for ecstasy, and he had decided to keep the money and not supply the pills.

They made an approach to Leon to remove this Dutch idiot from the picture. The idiot wore a chunky gold medallion around his neck and wore a gold Rolex on his wrist, and to finish the look he had a ponytail. Most Dutch low-class, low-life criminals had ponytails, so that summed him up nicely.

When I say out 'of the picture', we are not talking death here, but simply to provide enough persuasion to make him to think twice about maintaining any level of contact with the gang from Manchester.

I knew there was something in the offing but, as

I didn't need to be involved in any of the negotiations, I just carried on about my business and waited for the inevitable call to be made to me.

As it happened, one of our favourite haunts was a brothel called the Pompidou. The owner loved having us hanging around as she knew there would never be any trouble, and the police wouldn't drop by or certainly not stay if they saw any of us. Rumour had it the Madam was an ex-girlfriend of Leon, but we didn't hold that against her.

As I wasn't in the loop with the whys and wherefores, I simply turned up at the Pompidou early one evening, having received a message from Leon.

I looked my usual suave self as I entered the bar area. It must have looked quite surreal to those unfamiliar with the place. There was a man playing a piano in full suit and tie and, just above him on the wall, was a huge television playing porn. No one was paying a great deal of attention to anything, and the mood was good. I wandered over towards one end of the bar near to where Chris was buying one of the regular girls' champagne.

On a casual glance around the bar, it looked as though there were about eight of the gang all busy chatting, drinking and generally not looking as though we knew each other.

All the girls knew who we were and, while none

of them showed any recognition of us, you could sense that the more of us who turned up, the happier they were. Of course, if anything did go down, we could rely on them to deny seeing anything.

Just as an aside, should you ever find yourself in a brothel at the end of the night, you'll notice the carpets are all absolutely soaking. The girls don't want to get drunk, they just want the punters' money, so they surreptitiously tip the champagne away and invariably get another poured for them at an exorbitant price to the client.

Chris nodded to the barman and bought yet another glass for one of his favourite girls.

Behind me I heard the word 'cunt', but Chris tipped me the wink that the word had been intended for him. I twitched. There were four farmers standing close behind me, all trying to get a look in with the girl Chris was chatting to and, clearly, having very little success. As I leaned into the bar to pick up my drink, Chris whispered that none of the farmers were our target and to relax, so I relaxed.

The champagne was subtly poured away after a small sip by the working girl, so Chris ordered another.

'Cunt,' said the man behind me again.

Now, when a person I don't know calls my good friend this name once that's bad enough, but twice, well that's just taking the piss.

In one swift movement I jolted my elbow back which hit him squarely in the face, displacing his nose by forty-five degrees, I swivelled as he slumped against the wall and slowly sunk to the floor. I lifted my knee which met perfectly with his chin with such force that he actually made his way back up the wall.

His goading friend was now in a headlock thanks to Buck, who I heard saying to his new friend, that if he didn't move, I wouldn't hit him. He didn't move. I hit him. Several teeth fell to the floor just ahead of him hitting the deck and, with a half twist, I brought my hand back and inadvertently punched the target we were in the brothel to batter.

With my adrenaline soaring and forward momentum, I smashed my fist with such force, I honestly thought Mr. Necklace would find himself in the middle of next week.

Bugger me, all he did was shake his head as if trying to remove an irritating fly. I thought I'd better hit him again but missed. How the hell could I miss? Mick had slipped behind him and knocked his legs away, so I swung a second time and Mr. Necklace started on a downward trajectory. As he went down, Hans came up, grinning like a fool, brandishing a Rolex on one wrist, a new Rolex on the other, and a shiny new gold medallion around his neck. After that, all hell broke loose.

The girls sidled away, and the remaining farmers made a very quick exit. Madam Pompidou strolled over to the pianist, who played on regardless. In fact, I could swear I caught him playing 'Eye of the Tiger' from *Rocky III*. Good man.

We ended up outside and the last I recall was Chris pointing a Heckler and Koch, capable of nineteen shots in one squeeze of the trigger, against our man's head, which was now distinctly lacking in gold. Chris made an idle threat about what might happen if he was ever seen in the area again or bothered those nice men from Manchester. He obviously clearly understood what we meant. Well, maybe 'idle' threat isn't quite accurate, but you get the gist.

Chris's golden tones worked because we never heard or saw anything of him again but, the best outcome of all, was that the farmers were banned from the Pompidou for causing trouble. Now you can't say fairer than that.

Chapter Thirty-Three

By now the massive heist of removing five tons of hash from a police warehouse was a vicious rumour flying around. This was mainly because it couldn't be substantiated.

The humiliation the police felt, both for having to release the drug dealer they had wanted in custody for years, and also the sheer volume of evidence stolen, was enough to set tongues wagging.

So great was the embarrassment, that the police commissioner of the region had put an injunction on all press releases. There might have been an inch column in the local paper the week following the robbery, but that was about it.

Nevertheless, rumours were rife, and our gang gained something of a celebrity status. Leon was desperately trying to become a star and loved the notoriety. We just let him get on with it. Despite the unfortunate nickname that we had given him, we would have hated our little retard to be picked on by other big bullies.

Leon and his wife had decided to have a night out

at a club in the market place in the centre of town. He had a Somalian bodyguard with him but, having reached the front of the queue, he was refused entry. When he enquired as to why, the large bouncer who was blocking his entry simply told him, because 'he' said so.

The bouncer knew who Leon was. He wanted to humiliate him and to send a message to the rest of our gang. Apparently, he was hoping to become part of a new team who were convinced they were going to take over from us.

Leon decided to call a meeting to explain the situation and ask us what we thought we should do. We came up with a plan, and throughout the following week made an approach to twenty reasonably small-time, but respected, criminals to ask for their assistance. No one refused our request, and we got their total support.

They were told to turn up at the Green Butterfly café bar, sometime between nine and ten that Saturday night. Ideally, they should wear a vest if they had one, but they were to bring absolutely no weapons. This last instruction couldn't have been emphasised enough.

Everyone turned up in casual clothes and sensible boots. I, however, decided to wear a smart pair of leather-soled shoes. I mean, after all, it was a Saturday night, and we were going out on the town.

Over about twenty minutes everyone turned up, ordered drinks and chatted away, having a lovely time.

Gathering so many criminals under one roof was bound to get the attention of the police. So it was no surprise when I entered and noticed two men sitting at the bar, clearly not part of the crowd. From a hundred feet you could see that they were undercover cops. Short of putting a blue light on their heads they couldn't have been more obvious. Even worse for them, they didn't have the intelligence to hide the guns they were packing.

Once everyone had arrived, Chris decided to approach the men and pat them down. He asked if they were policemen while he was doing this and, would you believe it, they decided to leave the café.

The good news was that the bar couldn't have been bugged because the cops had been there to try and hear what was going down.

Only our gang knew the plan, so we started to share the strategy. We had done some asking around in the week since Leon's refusal into the club. We discovered that many people had had bad experiences with the bouncers, including being beaten up for no apparent reason. These bouncers seemed to think that flexing their muscles and scaring people would help cement their reputation and, what was worse, was that they were claiming to be Legionnaires.

We flexed our muscles.

From the Green Butterfly you could see the door of another nightclub with bouncers outside, but our prime target was the club that Leon had been refused entry the previous weekend. It was about a hundred meters away and we sauntered up in small groups. The bouncers were expecting us, but were too stupid to realise they had already allowed Moon in. He had deliberately not met us at the cafe.

I led the group with Verdun, casually passing people in the queue. As soon as the bouncers spotted us, we started to run towards them. Being the big chickens they were, they turned on their heels and ran inside the nightclub.

We chased them onto the dance floor where Moon was already kicking in the head of an off-duty policeman, using his newly polished steel-toe-capped cowboy boots. The dance floor cleared as if a nuclear bomb had gone off.

All the exits were covered by the gang members of our newly formed criminal band. The dance floor was miraculously clear of people and, much as I tried, I couldn't get a punch in anywhere. Verdun was a master of Pencak, an Indonesian martial art. With incredible ease, he swiped and kicked his way through all the bouncers and anyone else working at the club, or generally in his way.

Moon, by now, had the copper on the floor but, despite his awkward position, he had managed to get his gun out and fire one shot into the ceiling.

We all fled. No one knew if another shot would come, or from where, so we dashed out as all the metal shutters started coming down behind us. I glanced behind to see two uniformed policemen handcuffing Moon and one of the other criminals, so the pair of them were effectively trapped inside.

There really is safety and strength in numbers. We were a huge pack of angry violent men, so we stuck together outside the club demanding that they release our guys. We had a cordon of about ten policemen in uniform behind us. They were communicating with the police inside the club about the unrest outside. Under intense pressure, they unlocked the cuffs and let our men go. Imagine the humiliation. We had forced the police to let go brutal, sadistic and wanted blokes.

Moon later told me the police inside the club had them pressed up against the roller shutters, guaranteeing that if the shooting started, then those in handcuffs would take the bullets first.

We all sauntered back down to the Green Butterfly and ordered more drinks. Buck and I were still frustrated. We had been heavily involved in the fight, but because of the genius moves Verdun performed, we hadn't actually thrown a punch. We decided to pop along to the other club nearby.

We walked past the considerable doors and, as we drew level with the bouncers, Buck shouted 'boo'. They both jumped back and emitted a nervous giggle like the first-class clowns they were, minus the red nose and big clown shoes. We continued for a few metres and turned back, with Buck repeating 'boo' a second time. On this occasion they didn't flinch but giggled like girls.

The third time, as soon as they came into view, we started running towards them at full pelt. The bouncers slammed the huge doors shut behind them as they started running through the building. The doors were about two and a half metres tall and fifteen centimetres thick. Buck kicked them mid-run, smashing them open. His strides didn't falter as we both ran through the building and out the other side. The bouncers split up, so I turned to the left behind one, while Buck turned right.

I ran around the back of another building near some woods and, as I skirted the corner, I saw the bouncer run straight through a two-deep line of armed military police holding shields. My leather-soled shoes had no grip and, as I tried to come to a halt, I skidded like Daffy Duck running straight into Elmer Fudd during duck season. I somehow turned myself around and went in search of Buck at full speed. I looked like I was running backwards but standing still.

I caught a glimpse of Buck sprinting into a pool club. This was a popular hangout for students and, while a few of them were dotted around the whole room, there were six sitting together and drinking coffee halfway down the bar. Behind the bar, one of the club bouncers was trying to arm himself. The pool club security man had a Doberman on a lead and was protecting the bouncer by blocking the bar entrance, with the dog keeping Buck at bay. I was five seconds behind, read the situation and did a running leap straight over the bar, landing on the bouncer who softened my blow and remained on the floor. As I was doing this, I shouted to the people in the club to get their heads down, so they couldn't witness anything.

I picked up a bar stool and started smashing it across the bouncer's head. After a few accurate hits, the Doberman ran out of the door in the opposite direction to me. I didn't let up with the stool but, in the commotion, the bouncer took out a small Swiss army knife with a two-inch blade and stabbed me. I moved one hand to my lower back where I had felt something hit my protective vest and discovered the knife. A new, fresh red mist descended.

I gestured to Buck to take over and, as I dropped the stool, I grabbed the neck of the security bloke and pinned him against a wall. He started punching my face, which just made me laugh, but his strength was weakening as the life blood was leaving him. He started to turn blue, just as I heard Leon shouting to me to let him go because he was one of ours. I let go immediately.

He slumped to the floor gasping for breath, looking pitifully grateful for Leon's timing. Apparently, he was a local copper, working a night shift as security, for extra money and his name was Sven. Well, you live and learn.

I then raised my arm to shoulder level and did a semi-circle arch of the club, pointing my finger and declaring to the students, that they had seen nothing, but I had seen them.

No one reported the incident. Someone called an ambulance, and the bouncer was gathered up and taken to hospital for a couple of weeks. I did hear that he made a full recovery.

We were never refused entry into any nightclubs again.

Within a week word got out to us that the police had severely beaten Leon's Somalian bodyguard and broken his jaw. We believe this was because of his association with Leon and, I suspect, for the humiliation we had caused them by our intimidation when we had forced them to un-cuff and release our gang members. And of course when, a few weeks earlier, we had successfully stolen five tons of hash from under their noses.

Within three weeks of this brawl, every single person involved got arrested for affray regarding the evening's events. It was stated that the good citizens of our small town had been offended by our actions. The police did dawn raids, but they did not arrest Buck or me.

To this day I have absolutely no idea why not.

They kept every one of our gang in for questioning for about three weeks. Every day Buck and I would phone all the police stations where they were being held to check that no one was harming a hair on their heads. Nothing beats intimidating the police to get your day off to a good start. The whole gang ended up with a week in prison and a few hours of community service, but the police still had egg on their faces.

Chapter Thirty-Four

With some of the money I had accrued, I decided to buy myself a boat. It was jolly useful to be living within a jet-ski ride of the shore and, if any police decided to rock up and try and see what I was up to from their position on dry land, I could simply raise the anchor and sail away to another convenient spot. Naturally, I allowed the police to complete setting up their surveillance equipment first, then I'd weigh anchor and drift away. It was worth it just to see their annoyance.

One particular day, I had some guns that I needed to drop off at the boat, which I had moored on the Maas River. Mick and I were going for a night out with a couple of delightful women so, to reduce the risk of any trouble, we thought we'd better drop the guns off first, before heading into town.

Mick was driving, with me as front passenger, and the girls were in the back. He decided to take a route through a wood which was a well-known area for gay men to meet.

Just as we exited the wood, within sight of my boat, we saw a man standing on the side of the path holding on to his moped.

It became obvious that Mick and this man knew each other, mainly because Mick, being a gypsy, hated gays, and gays, as a result, tended to hate Mick. His idea of fun was to wind them up and, if possible, to physically hurt them. Unfortunately, as Mick drove past him, the moped man leant forward and spat on the windscreen.

That was not a clever move.

Mick slammed on the brakes and reversed the car over the moped. I told the girls to drop into the foot wells and not move until I said so. I then leapt from the car to fold up the number plate.

In Holland number plates are made of aluminium so they are easy to bend, and we couldn't run the risk of a random person witnessing a disagreement and making a note of our number plate.

Mick then drove back over the moped, which was now a complete write-off, and leapt from the car. The man, clearly furious about his moped being completely destroyed, had grabbed his crook lock and smashed it with huge force across Mick's chest. Mick grabbed the man and started hitting him as if striking a punch bag. This lasted for about five minutes and ended with the man being thrown into a hedge, quickly followed by his flat moped.

We then carried on, dropped the guns off on my boat, straightened the number plate and went to have a delightful meal in town. We then went for a bit of a dance at a local club, where the charming bouncers were delighted to allow us entry.

The following morning, Mick's dad received a call from the police in Oosterhout, asking him to tell his son to pop in and have a word with them. Apparently, someone had complained that the night before he had been beaten up and his moped destroyed.

Mick called me and I happily agreed to drive him down to the police station. En route we discussed how we would explain our perspective on the previous night's events. Once we had our stories straight, I parked at the back of the police station, opened the newspaper I'd brought with me and sat back to catch up with the day's news.

It was about half an hour later when my mobile rang. I had put in my English SIM card so, when the policeman called, he genuinely thought he was ringing an English mobile.

The copper asked me if I had been hitch-hiking the day before and if I'd accepted a lift from anyone. I explained that I had. Then the policeman asked me if there was any possibility that I could come to the police station. I asked where he was and, when he said Oosterhout police station, I explained that, by happy coincidence, I happened to be in Oosterhout town centre and that if he could hang on for half an hour, I'd be happy to pop in.

I went back to the paper and thirty minutes later, dressed in typically British garb, I strolled into the police reception. I was warmly greeted and thanked, then taken to an interview room and then asked to recall what had happened the previous evening.

I explained that my car had broken down while I was on my way to a marina where my boat was moored. I hadn't realised it was so far to walk so I had decided to try and hitch a lift as there were no cabs around. After a while a man stopped. He was, by coincidence, heading for the harbour so I accepted a lift. I went on further to explain that we had just passed through some woods as a short cut when, out of nowhere, a man stepped forward and spat on the car windscreen. I said I was really quite shocked because it was completely unexpected and totally unprovoked.

Then the driver giving me a lift, whose name I didn't recall, got out of his car to face the man and question his actions. I couldn't see what the provocateur was holding, but it looked like a metal object and, without pausing or saying anything, he had smacked this metal bar or whatever it was, across the driver's chest.

At this point I demonstrated with my hand

whereabouts Mick had been hit. I then added that it might have been something like a crook lock that he was hit with.

The copper's face was a mixture of surprise and disappointment as I had recalled almost exactly what Mick had said. The events that had unfolded the night before clearly seemed to have been initiated by the moped owner.

The police had no choice but to release Mick. Before doing so, the police officer took me quietly to one side and asked me if I knew who Mick was. I said I didn't, and what did it matter, he was a kind person who had stopped and given me a much-needed lift.

The policeman discreetly took my elbow and, in almost hushed tones, he explained that Mick was a highly dangerous and violent man who was very well known to the police in the district. On top of that he was part of a notorious, almost infamous, gang in Holland that had caused untold grief to the local community.

I delivered a stunning performance; I mean RADA would have been proud. I had a panicked look in my eyes while simultaneously taking a long step backwards. While I did this, I touched the policeman's forearm and asked him if I could have been in any personal danger. He responded that he strongly advised me to be much more careful before accepting lifts from strangers, especially while I was in a foreign country.

We could not have got away with it today. There were no computer links between police forces, and communication was mainly through phone calls, so no one could easily check up on any individual. It obviously didn't occur to the policeman to check me out at the next nearest police station which happened to be only ten kilometres down the road. Officers there would have known me and my track record very well.

No, as far as that copper was concerned, I was an Englishman enjoying a few weeks' holiday on my boat and sailing around Europe.

The relevant paperwork was signed, and Mick was released, grinning broadly. As we walked away, I put my arm across his shoulder, while looking over mine at the astonished officer. In Holland, once a person has been released after being questioned, and not prosecuted, that person could not be charged again for the same crime.

In perfect Dutch I told him that Mick was my best friend.

You could almost see the steam of anger emanating from him. He had been totally duped. But at least he could tell his grandchildren that he'd been duped by some of the best gangsters in the business.

Chapter Thirty-Five

Leon was becoming more of a muppet, which made him something of a liability, because our reputation was growing. We all wanted to guard our anonymity as the fewer people who knew what we looked like, the greater our chances of surprise and success. Leon needed to be dealt with, and the opportunity came from a tip given to Mick.

Just as an aside, one of the things we ensured was that we never took any group photos. Even though the police knew that we knew each other and worked with one another, it is incredibly hard to prove if you haven't got a picture of us all together. In fact, if my memory serves me well, I believe Leon owns the only photo of us all at one of his weddings. Whether he still has it or not, I have no idea.

The fame and notoriety that Leon was attracting was becoming increasingly dangerous to us. He had rented a bungalow on the outskirts of town and was using it to grow marijuana, which in itself wasn't the end of the world, but for a while now he hadn't been sticking to the gang rules. He was rapidly becoming a danger to us as a whole, without seeming bothered by the possible consequences of his behaviour. He only seemed to care about his reputation, which he saw as being a tough guy and team leader. He was no more a leader than I was a Bolshoi ballerina.

We found out about the house and his planting venture by accident. Had he not been acting suspiciously, we probably wouldn't have discovered what he was up to. When you are part of a gang, you cannot help but become an incredibly tight-knit group. Our success was based on honesty between us, no matter how unpleasant it might be. Leon didn't seem to care that he could be putting us in jeopardy, all because of his personal greed.

Bizarrely, the bungalow he had rented and in which he had planted about fifteen hundred plants, was being tended to by a local gypsy. I mean, how stupid can you get?

Mick was incredibly well-respected, but his reputation had taken years of hard work and trust to establish, he always had his ear to the ground, and Leon knew this.

Almost every day people would approach him. One day, another gypsy had mentioned to him that his friend was looking after a plantation for Leon. I mean, really?

It wasn't beyond the wit of man to track this

person down so, a few days later, we followed him from his home to a local supermarket. Nothing suspicious in that, except he didn't strike us as the kind of man who would do the weekly shop.

In Holland these places have many exits and are usually in the middle of a huge car park. So our man parked his car and waited a few minutes as he looked around to check he had not been followed. Then he walked from his car into the supermarket and straight out the other side. He sauntered over to a little red runabout, and drove off followed by myself and Jamal, straight to Leon's rented bungalow.

Now Jamal was a horrible, arrogant, smelly little git. He stank so badly, we had to drive with the car windows open. Seriously. He could not understand how he never had a girlfriend. As if that wasn't bad enough, he was also an untalented wanker. I didn't like him. He had come into the gang when he was twenty-one. We had spent time teaching him the tricks of the trade but, whenever he had money, he got a big mouth. It wasn't long before we realised just what an ungrateful, untrustworthy pig he was. When I heard of his death in 2003, long after the gang had disbanded, I actually had a couple of drinks to celebrate.

Mick contacted me about his demise. Apparently, he had taken on a man in his early twenties as his chauffeur. It just so happened that this young driver was the only son of a very wealthy and influential man.

The pair of them were in France when something happened, which resulted in Jamal shooting dead his driver. The father caught up with Jamal, his brother, Ahmed, and a friend in a café in Tangier. He shot them with a machine pistol. This is an auto-loading pistol capable of fully automatic fire, so effectively a handgun-style submachine gun.

His brother was hit first, but didn't die, whereas Jamal and their friend were killed instantly. Ahmed made a full recovery. However, weeks later, he was making a call from a phone box in Holland when the father caught up with him and made good his plan to take revenge on all the men who had killed his only child.

Anyway, we now knew where Leon's bungalow was located. As we had been given the heads up on his antics, we had planned to simply set fire to it, so everything inside would be destroyed.

Once the gypsy had done his work and was well out of the way, we parked out of sight of the bungalow and made our approach. Being the ever-prepared man, I had already made a Molotov cocktail knowing that just the one, thrown well, should do the trick.

The bungalow looked completely unassuming

and you wouldn't have realised what was being grown inside. With pinpoint accuracy, I threw the cocktail at one of the windows. However it had been impossible to see that the windows were boarded up on the inside.

The bottle broke on impact but bounced far enough back to land on Jamal who was standing near the window, and the petrol set him alight. He ran around in a frenzy, making some ungodly noise, so quick as a flash, I rugby tackled him to the ground and rolled him in the grass until he was merely a smouldering mass.

In this confusion, Jamal lost his gun, a Zastava CZ99 semi-automatic pistol. He didn't realise it at the time because the greatest priority was to leave the premises as we were drawing unwanted attention. We fled. Obviously, the noise and partial fire had caused neighbours to alert the fire service, so even though we didn't get the satisfaction of seeing the whole place go up in smoke, we knew it would be shut down by the police once the cannabis was discovered.

Luckily, neither the fire service nor the police found Jamal's gun while they were there. However, Leon did. Understandably, he instantly recognised who it belonged to and realised that his loss of business had to be an inside job. Don't get me wrong, we did not do this out of meanness or jealously, we just wanted rid of him. He wanted fame and notoriety while we just wanted the anonymity to make, sell and steal drugs for money.

As you might imagine, once Leon realised that some of the team weren't particularly happy with his antics, he distanced himself, and started making new plans for his future. We weren't stupid. As tips came to us, we still worked together and planned, but the rot was beginning to set in.

Chapter Thirty-Six

A couple of months later we had managed to sell most of the ecstasy tablets we had taken from the chemists and our last bag, stashed in a cupboard, was just about to be sold, so Mick and I decided to make some more.

Mick was an expert at making pills and he was prepared to show me what to do. It's not just the process, but the proportions that are vital to get right. We might be part of a gang, but we had a reputation to uphold, and we weren't going to shatter it by making shoddy pills. Our rules about not killing people extended to everyone, including everyday people who wanted to party and take some ecstasy.

Not only were we meticulous but George Henshaw, who was still Mr. Ecstasy in Holland, would randomly check batches to ensure the consistency of the quality. He also had a reputation to uphold, so he wasn't going to let pills made by a gang he trusted be released onto the market without inspection.

So having got the equipment we needed, we had to find somewhere to make the pills. Moon came up with a secluded place where he sometimes went on holiday. It was a chalet situated in a quiet woodland area which was part of a holiday complex popular with tourists. It was under an hour's drive from our town and he rented it for a week in his name.

We had to hire a three-and-a-half-ton tail-lift transit van to transport the pill machine, pallet jack and cement mixer, as they were too big and heavy to fit into our cars.

Buck and Hans collected the van which Buck had hired in his own name. He picked it up on a Friday morning and then collected me as I was the only one who knew where the pill machine had been stored. Then he drove me to the weekend retreat.

Being a flat country, you could see for miles and, as we made our way in the van, we could see in the distance and slightly to our right that a helicopter was hovering. It occasionally ducked below the horizon, but it was clearly keeping an eye on what seemed to be the only van on the road. When we reached the chalet, you could hear the sound of it fading away. We were pretty sure they now knew where we were, although not necessarily the exact chalet. However, they would be second guessing what we might be getting up to.

You have to give the police some credit. It didn't

take much to work out that, when two gang members drive a hire van to a secluded area not far from their home town, something must be afoot. We suspected that the van hire company had tipped the wink to the police, thinking they might be interested.

We reached the chalet mid-morning and unloaded the pill-making machine, cement mixer and milk powder. We closed all the internal doors, put the heating on and slightly opened a window to allow any excess moisture out. This ensured that we would come back to a completely dry room, which is the ideal condition to make the pills.

We locked up the chalet and returned the hired van. The police would know roughly where we had headed that morning, so we couldn't take the risk of the van being traced to the chalet.

I collected my car while Mick, who had the remaining ingredients needed to make the pills, drove straight back to the chalet.

Mick had told me how to make the pills, so I started with a small run just to make sure I'd got the ratios right. Mick did not believe in this placebo nonsense so, as soon as I had made a few, he swallowed one.

They were too dense as I'd over-egged something and Mick needed to work out exactly and quickly, what I had done wrong. Between us the corrections were made and, twenty minutes later,

Mick was out for the count. He came to periodically, and we held quite sensible conversations, even making plans to start edging away from the gang.

He and I were taking all the risks and doing the work, while the others were pissing it up and enjoying the spoils from our productivity.

I manufactured pills all night while Mick slept like a baby. Luckily, he woke, more or less when I'd finished, so he started cleaning the room and helped me pack the ecstasy.

We placed the pills in doubled-up bin-liners and put them in doubled-up cardboard boxes, as this made them easier to carry. Overnight I had manufactured a little over a million ecstasy pills. The only things we left in the immaculately clean room were the cement mixer, pill machine and a dustpan and brush which held a tiny amount of MDMA from the floor sweepings.

However, there was still a lot of dust everywhere as a result of the manufacturing, so the plan was to return to completely sanitise the room and collect what we couldn't lift on Monday. We had cleared the whole room of our fingerprints and were driving away from the chalet by eight-thirty on Saturday morning.

Mick had pre-located an American camper van in a caravan camp site and we stashed the pills inside the bunk seating for safe keeping.

The Dutch police force knew we were gang members and had camera evidence from the helicopter as to our probable location. However, instead of doing a raid on Friday night when they spotted us, they went home to their families and enjoyed a delightful evening. They stormed the house Saturday morning at about half past nine. There's probably a moral in there somewhere.

Had I not cocked up the first batch that Mick had swallowed, we would have probably started making the pills on Saturday morning. However, with him flat out, once I had the correct ratios, it just made sense to get on with it and get the pills made. Consequently, none of the gang were expecting myself and Mick back so soon, so it seemed a perfect opportunity to stir things up for Leon.

We 'borrowed', on a fairly permanent basis, a Nissan Primera GT with a red top engine. A good pikey friend of Mick broke into it using a slim jim lock pick. He got around the central locking system, despite there being an immobiliser, and got it started in seconds. I tell you, it was bloody impressive to watch.

It was about two-thirty in the morning when we reached the crescent where Leon lived. In this particular area the houses, and their allotted parking spaces, were separated by a road, so a reasonable distance apart.

Leon's car was parked in a bay directly opposite his house. I had managed to pick up a percussion grenade. This had a completely smooth casing with a pin on the top and was basically an 'easy to throw' bomb. It had a less destructive force and created a much smaller explosion than other grenades, so it was an ideal weapon to blow up a car. It was activated when thrown, and so loud that anyone near to the explosion would become deaf for a period of time.

Mick drove the Primera, while I lay in the back seat foot well, as it made it easier to roll the grenade under Leon's car from twenty feet away. As you can imagine, once the pin was released and I'd spun it along the ground, we had to get away really quickly, so we didn't get caught in the shrapnel.

It was a perfect pitch and the car bent like a banana. The grenade left an enormous crater and blew out every single window of the surrounding houses. Leon's neighbours had wanted him to leave well before this incident as they knew he was attracting trouble, so this was the final straw, not just for him, but for the rest of the gang.

The success of our gang depended on our anonymity. We were known to the police, but not to the general public. The cops needed to keep a lid on things, because they wanted to catch us in a huge publicity sting. They realised that we kept other villains in check and they also knew we were hard to place together, uncommunicative between one another and with no obvious pre-planning to our operations.

Leon started making accusations that Mick and I were behind the bombing, claiming he had seen the back of my car leaving the scene on the evening of the explosion. The car we had stolen for the job was a different make, model and colour to mine, so we knew he was talking complete bollocks.

Chris told us that Leon was on the warpath, so we thought we'd pay him a visit and try to put his mind at rest and reassure him it wasn't us.

As it happened, Mick had to attend an important family meeting, so I was hanging around his place while he showered and dressed. We intended to visit Leon first, before Mick went to his gathering. Mick was wearing an expensive sharp suit and tie, with highly polished designer shoes.

The plan was to spend a few minutes with Leon, and then I would drop Mick off around the corner. Not long into our journey I stopped at a red light in a right-hand lane, indicating that I was going to turn right. Just as the lights turned green, a junkie cycled in front of the car, one hand on his handlebars, the other holding up his middle finger at me.

I wasn't going to stand for this gesticulation and, as I watched him cycle down the path running parallel to the road I'd just driven up, I slammed the car into reverse for fifty metres and leapt out. I grabbed the junkie's t-shirt at the neck and slammed him up against a tree.

In the meantime, Mick was jumping all his considerable bulk on the bicycle and letting air out of his tyres. Out of nowhere, an Astra containing two men came to a halt. One of the men leapt out and pushed me to the floor. I let him hit me because I didn't know if it was the police or not. Mick shouted that they weren't coppers, so I hit him one almighty punch while simultaneously leaping to my feet. Out of the corner of my eye I saw Mick hit the Astra's passenger through his open window.

I let the junkie go and turned to find ten Royal Marechaussee standing in the road. Believe you me, you do not want to be facing these guys, unless they are on your side but, by the look of them, they obviously weren't on ours.

The Royal Netherlands Marechaussee is the national gendarmerie force, making up one of the two national police and armed forces. This lot were from the military academy over the road.

Clearly, they were ready to pile in so, with everyone we'd hit now out of the way, Mick and I faced them square on. Even though we were greatly outnumbered, they looked nervous of us and started to back off. In that split second we ran back to my car.

In the meantime the Astra had moved to block our path. In that instant, the junkie raced to my car and, with great force, kicked a huge dent in the side of the door. I did a handbrake turn, floored it and managed to drive around the Astra. I drove for a couple of hundred meters up the wrong side of the street and dropped Mick off.

I called Chris to find out where he was and, luckily, he was having breakfast with his wife in a nearby restaurant. Knowing exactly where they were located, I ran in and left my gun with her. While she stayed and finished breakfast, Chris and I drove to the local police station to hand ourselves in.

When you are a violent gang member you cannot afford to give the police any opportunity to get a search warrant or to be wanted for arrest, so it is always best to confront the situation. Which is why, fifteen minutes after the incident, Chris and I strolled into the local nick.

It was like a scene out of *Hill Street Blues.* There was complete pandemonium. The men from the Astra were shouting and waving their hands, several street witnesses were strongly voicing their opinions, and the junkie was yelling and holding up part of his destroyed bike, while the small-town cop was trying to keep order.

I thought I'd add to the confusion by saying that

I was the one who had been accosted first and that they were all in on it. To silence the melee Chris shouted, 'You are all gonna to die', which arguably is true, but the undertone of his roaring sounded like a real threat and made everyone stop for a second. In the far corner stood a prosecutor, who pointed to me and shouted, 'Pommie, cells!'

A policeman escorted me to the only cell downstairs, locking the door behind me. It was two metres square with a bench. I sat down and called my lawyer. I mean we are talking small-town coppers here. I wasn't searched for drugs, guns or phones, and I could clearly overhear someone saying that they were going to move me to a larger police station. So when I called our lawyer, who was probably one of the most corrupt solicitors in Holland, I told him to make his way to the station I expected to be at in probably half an hour.

Just as I finished the call, an officer walked into my cell, and without hesitation I handed my phone over to him, saying it had run out of battery anyway.

This solicitor represented the whole gang and was called whenever one of us got into trouble. His number was the only one we kept on our mobiles, so the police had nothing should our phones be taken.

They had to let Chris go for two reasons; first he clearly wasn't the man the witnesses saw with me, and second there was only one cell, which I was currently occupying.

I was questioned about an alleged assault and kept in custody for three days. By the time I was released, Leon had calmed down and was no longer making accusations, and Mick had moved the ecstasy to another safe place. He told me where it was. He only trusted me, so didn't share this information with any other gang member.

A few months after this incident Leon moved to Spain, not a moment too soon.

Chapter Thirty-Seven

The gang really did have a good reputation that we were fair and always kept to our word.

It must have been three weeks after our break-in to remove the apricot tins that we heard that Dom had been killed. We were sad to hear this news. He'd left a widow and two small children and all because he assumed he had got away with it and ignored our precautionary advice.

You can't tell some people and Dom was one of them. He had invested a year in showing me where the warehouses were and he felt he deserved to be well rewarded once the hash had been successfully taken. He did not take in the fact that, up to that point, he had actually been incredibly lucky.

It had been sheer fluke that his bosses had asked him to step in at the last minute. Sheer fluke that we weren't on another job and could drop everything to reach Antwerp docks. It was sheer fluke that the container holding the hash had been taken to a nearby police station, and sheer fluke that there were no alarms, CCTV, guards or surveillance watching the police warehouse. But most of all, it was sheer fluke that the warehouse was made of wood.

After a few weeks, we managed to track his wife down. She had decided to remain in Holland, but well away from the district where she had lived with Dom. We waited until she was settled and then handed over the remaining twenty-five percent cash that we had agreed to. She was set for life, but somehow we got the feeling she would rather have had her daft, dyslexic husband back than all that money.

I am aware that, despite all the rip deals we carried out, by far the greatest achievement for us was the humiliation we caused to the Dutch police by removing hash with a street value of the equivalent of twenty-five million pounds, right from under their noses. I believe this remains the largest robbery from the police in the world.

THE END

Epilogue

As the new century approached, the gang started to break up. Some got arrested for taking or selling Class As, some got caught doing a job, some were nabbed for aggravated assault or murder and some were killed.

Modern technology, naturally, signalled the beginning of the end.

The press didn't want to show too much admiration for the gang because they probably didn't want to encourage others, or make the gang look glamourous. However, these are some of the comments the media wrote about them, at the time.

'This gang formed a motley crew of criminals'

'Looked like a local commando unit than a regular crime ring'

'This group was characterized by an extraordinary professionalism and degree of organisation'

'The organization is suspected of a long series of kidnappings, extortion, drug robbery (rip deals), aggravated assault and the production and trade in XTC'

At one point, a judiciary described us as *'a state in the state'*

'The court case was well reported and gripped the nation for weeks on end. However the prison sentences, which were expected to be a minimum of eighteen years, came to nothing in the end because Pommie, who was the crucial key witness, had the case swept aside by the Court of Appeal, because he was able to prove that a Public Prosecutor had lied under oath.'

It's definitely the simple things in life that make it so rich, and I have fond memories of being in court, running the cassette around in my hand that had the recorded proof that Public Prosecutor had lied. Once played to the judge we knew we would be free men.

In 2016, Leon decided to make a short film. In it he is seen driving a nice car, with ambitions to be a local politician. He clearly knew it would draw attention to him. He loved the notoriety that being a gang member brought, especially when he believed he had been the leader of that gang.

In the film, he doesn't give much away and he actually denies that he was present at some of the deals that went down. But he cannot have it both ways, so I guess you'll have to make up your own mind.

Acknowledgements

Pommie, because *Hash* couldn't have been written without sharing your memories.

Helen Kewley and Jo Dutton for editing the book and Hendrick Sultana for the cover design.